People Around You

Lehrerhandbuch

Introduction to text types and working strategies for advanced learners

Hannspeter Bauer, Klaus Hinz, Angela Luz, Brigitte Prischtt, Stephen Speight

Edited by Klaus Hinz

New Edition

Schöningh

© 2007 Bildungshaus Schulbuchverlage
Westermann Schroedel Diesterweg Schöningh Winklers GmbH
Braunschweig, Paderborn, Darmstadt

www.schoeningh-schulbuch.de
Schöningh Verlag, Jühenplatz 1–3, 33098 Paderborn

Das Werk und seine Teile sind urheberrechtlich geschützt.
Jede Nutzung in anderen als den gesetzlich zugelassenen Fällen bedarf der vorherigen schriftlichen Einwilligung des Verlages.
Hinweis zu § 52a UrhG: Weder das Werk noch seine Teile dürfen ohne eine solche Einwilligung gescannt und in ein Netzwerk gestellt werden.
Das gilt auch für Intranets von Schulen und sonstigen Bildungseinrichtungen.

Auf verschiedenen Seiten dieses Buches befinden sich Verweise (Links) auf Internet-Adressen. Haftungshinweis: Trotz sorgfältiger inhaltlicher Kontrolle wird die Haftung für die Inhalte der externen Seiten ausgeschlossen. Für den Inhalt dieser externen Seiten sind ausschließlich deren Betreiber verantwortlich. Sollten Sie dabei auf kostenpflichtige, illegale oder anstößige Inhalte treffen, so bedauern wir dies ausdrücklich und bitten Sie, uns umgehend per E-Mail davon in Kenntnis zu setzen, damit beim Nachdruck der Verweis gelöscht wird.

Druck 5 4 3 2 1 / Jahr 2011 10 09 08 07
Die letzte Zahl bezeichnet das Jahr dieses Druckes.

Umschlaggestaltung: e-BILDWERKE, Kassel
Druck und Bindung: AZ Druck und Datentechnik, Kempten/Allgäu

ISBN 978-3-14-040009-1

Table of Contents

Vorwort 6
Vom Text zum Aufgabenapparat 7
Wortschatzarbeit 10
Prozessorientierte Schreibschulung 12

Decisive moments – Short story 14

Funktion und Aufbau des Kapitels 14
Introduction 15
Suspect shot by police dies 16
At two o'clock in the morning (Ernest Hemingway) 17
Just along for the ride (Dennis Kurumada) 20
Small avalanches (Joyce Carol Oates) 24
Thematic vocabulary 29

Klausurvorschlag   I used to live here once (Jean Rhys) 30

Additional text   Documentary photographs (Jerzy Kosinski) 32

Helpless and lonely – Drama 33

Funktion und Aufbau des Kapitels 33
Introduction 34
A helping hand (Playlet by Stephen Speight) 35
Hello out there! (Short play by William Saroyan) 39
Thematic vocabulary 50

Klausurvorschlag   Martha and Karen (A dramatic scene by Roger Karshner) 51

Additional text   The split decision (excerpt) (Short play by William Moseley) 54

All you need is love – Poetry 57

Funktion und Aufbau des Kapitels 57
Introduction 58
Central Park at dusk (Sara Teasdale) 58
The Passionate Shepherd to his love (Christopher Marlowe) 61

🎵 Comeclose and Sleepnow (Roger McGough) **64**
🎵 Serious luv (Benjamin Zephaniah) **68**
🎵 First love (John Clare) **71**
🎵 O when I was (A. E. Housman) **73**
🎵 Ending (Gavin Ewart) **76**
🎵 40 – Love (Roger McGough) **78**
Poor girl (Maya Angelou) **80**
Funeral Blues (W. H. Auden) **82**
To my son (Thomas Hood) **84**
For Heidi with blue hair (Fleur Adcock) **85**
For a good dog (Ogden Nash) **87**
Thematic vocabulary **88**

Klausurvorschlag I am very bothered (Simon Armitage) **89**

Where does Britain belong? – Non-fictional texts 91

Funktion und Aufbau des Kapitels **91**
Introduction **92**

Britain, America The British Dilemma (Anthony Sampson) **92**
and Europe Cartoon: 4 more years **94**

Britain and France Photo **96**
🎵 Bonjour mate (Helena Frith Powell) **97**
France's vision is not ours (Anatole Kaletsky) **99**

Britain and Germany Two kinds of spitfire **102**
British-German relations – two views: Old enemies – new friends? **104**
Stop making fun of the hun (Catherine Mayer) **104**
Kein Pardon. Der Queen-Besuch und das heikle deutsch-britische Verhältnis (Stefan Klein) **107**

Britain and Europe Map and verbal information, sample questions **110**
🎵 Only Labour values can take us forward in Europe (Gary Titley) **111**
Does Britain need Europe? **115**

Klausurvorschlag The British-American 'party' **117**

Additional texts The question of Britishness that even had the Palace stumped (Richard Ford) **121**
The UK entry quiz **123**
Ask the people **125**
Europe old and young (Stephen Speight) **125**

Reel or real? – A television series 127

Funktion und Aufbau des Kapitels 127
Introduction 128
Dawson's Creek: A very popular drama 130
Szenenprotokoll: Episode 1 131
Synopsis of Dawson's Creek: "Emotions in Motion" 134
Pre-credit sequence and opening credits 137
Part I: Newcomers in town 138
Part II: First day at Capeside High 143
Part III: A night at the movies 147
Part IV: The end of a night at the movies 151
Evaluating the film 154
Beyond the film 155
Appreciating a film: Reviews 155
Review of Clueless (Gabriela Toth) 156
Thematic vocabulary 158

Klausurvorschlag Dawson's Creek, episode 1: "Dawson walks Jen home" (Scene 30) 159

Acknowledgements 161

Vorwort

Das Hauptziel von *People Around You* besteht in der präzisen Erarbeitung der Spezifika nichtfiktionaler und literarischer Textsorten sowie filmischer Gestaltungsmittel, in der Einübung adäquater Lesarten und Erschließungstechniken sowie des Umgangs mit textbezogenem und metasprachlichem Vokabular. Das Buch ist sowohl für die Einführung in Textsorten und Analyseverfahren im fortgeschrittenen Englischunterricht der Sekundarstufe II als auch für spätere Wiederholungen und die Vorbereitung auf die Reifeprüfung konzipiert.

Dem übergreifenden Lernziel entspricht die textsortenbezogene Anordnung der Textkorpora in fünf thematisch angelegten Kapiteln einschließlich der Erweiterung themenbezogenen Vokabulars. Das Buch enthält folgende Kapitel:

1. Decisive moments – Short story
2. Helpless and lonely – Drama
3. All you need is love – Poetry
4. Where does Britain belong? – Non-fictional texts
5. Reel or real? – A television series

Anhang: "How to read texts – How to talk about texts – How to write texts".

Jedes Kapitel wird mit einer Zusammenfassung des thematischen Vokabulars in Bezugsfeldern und einer schematischen Darstellung der Analyse der betreffenden Textsorte abgeschlossen.

Im Rahmen der Verwirklichung der Lernziele „Textrezeption und Textproduktion" werden folgende Ziele verfolgt:

- Vorstellung unterschiedlicher Textformen und Textformvarianten:
  Die Schüler/innen gewinnen Einblick in unterschiedliche Textformen wie Kurzgeschichte, Drama, Gedicht, Film und Sachtext (Wissen um Texte).
- Einführung in Methoden der Interpretation fiktionaler und Analyse nichtfiktionaler und medial vermittelter Texte: Die Schüler/innen lernen Verfahren zur detaillierten und selektiven Erschließung von Textinhalten kennen (Methodenbeherrschung in Bezug auf Textrezeption).
- Einführung in Verfahren der Sprach- und Stilanalyse im Rahmen der Textarbeit:
  Die Schüler/innen lernen Formen der Sprachverwendung innerhalb eines Textes in Bezug auf Lexik und Textkonstitution kennen und beurteilen (Sprachreflektion).
- Erweiterung des Analyse- und Beschreibungsvokabulars:
  Die Schüler/innen erweitern schrittweise ihr Vokabular zur Interpretation und Analyse fiktionaler und nichtfiktionaler Texte sowie zur eigenen Texterstellung (textbezogene Wortschatzerweiterung).
- Erweiterung oberstufenadäquater Lern- und Arbeitstechniken:
  Die Schüler lernen Hilfen und Arbeitsverfahren kennen, mithilfe derer sie Texte erschließen und (re)produzieren können.

Vom Text zum Aufgabenapparat

Die Analyse und Interpretation von Texten durchläuft im Allgemeinen mehrere Stufen: die Vortextphase, die individuelle Textrezeption, die schülerorientierte Textbesprechung und die (schriftliche) Nachbereitung der Unterrichtsergebnisse.

1. Vortextphase

Die der Textarbeit vorgeschalteten Aktivitäten unterscheiden sich je nach Texttyp, Textform und Länge des zu besprechenden Textes beträchtlich.
Sachtexte beschreiben objektive Begebenheiten, die in der Textvorlaufphase zuweilen eine Aktivierung des Vorwissens seitens des Lesers bzw. eine Zulieferung notwendigen Vorwissens durch Kurztexte oder Lehrerinformationen erforderlich machen können.
Literarische Texte werden nicht als etwas objektiv Gegebenes verstanden, der Leser ist vielmehr an der Erschließung ihres Sinnes beteiligt. Am Anfang der Lektüre stehen die Erwartungen des Lesers an den Text, die den Leseprozess steuern. Dieser Prozess wird *top-down-Methode* genannt. Zur Intensivierung des Interaktionsprozesses zwischen Leser und Text und aus der Erkenntnis heraus, dass die Beschäftigung mit Literatur lernerorientierter vor sich gehen müsse, werden zunehmend neue Wege in Form von Übungen und Aktivitäten beschritten, die der Lektüre vorgeschaltet werden. Es wird angestrebt, Hintergrundwissen und lebensweltliches Vorwissen zu (re)aktivieren, Erwartungshaltungen aufzubauen und globale Voraussagen zum Inhalt des zu lesenden Textes zu entwickeln, die den Leser-Text-Dialog initiieren und den Leseprozess insgesamt steuern. Der Schüler wird dann beim Lesen von Zeit zu Zeit innehalten, um auf das bereits Gelesene zurückzublicken, er wird Voraussagen verifizieren oder falsifizieren und ggf. modifizieren.
In *People Around You* sind nicht explizit für jeden Text sog. *pre-reading* Aktivitäten ausgewiesen; es obliegt vielmehr dem erfahrenen Lehrer, entsprechende Hinweise zu geben bzw. die Schüler selbst einen adäquaten Zugang zum Text suchen zu lassen. Es bieten sich textinterne Stimuli (Textüberschrift, dem Text entnommene Abbildungen, Textanfang, Textteile usw.) oder textexterne Stimuli (textunabhängige Bilder, provokative Äußerungen, problem- oder themenbezogene Denkanstöße, Recherchen usw.) an.
Je nach Textart und didaktischem Ansatz lassen sich mit diesen Aktivitäten folgende Lernziele verfolgen:

- Sensibilisierung und Motivierung für die Thematik des Textes,
- (Re-)Aktivierung des lebensweltlichen Vorwissens,
- Bereitstellung des textlichen Hintergrundwissens,
- Entwicklung von Erwartungshaltungen.

2. Textrezeption

Vor Beginn des Leseprozesses sollte der methodische Leitfaden zur Textrezeption im *Appendix* des Schülerbuchs (*How to read texts*, S. 135f.) besprochen werden. Die Textrezeption wird in *People Around You* gelegentlich durch den Leseprozess steuernde, vorwärtsweisende *while-reading*-Aufgaben im Sinne eines *guided reading* unterstützt. Die Schüler/innen erhalten in der Randspalte Anleitungen, beim Lesen ausgewählter Passagen bestimmte Phänomene zu beachten (cf. Students' Book, S. 12); sie sollen die gewonnenen Erkenntnisse dann als Stütze für die schülerorientierte

Auseinandersetzung mit dem Text im Plenum schriftlich festhalten bzw. bei längeren Texten ein *reading log* führen (cf. Students' Book S. 136). Obwohl davon auszugehen ist, dass Schüler/innen der Sekundarstufe II die Führung eines *reading log* am Ende der Sekundarstufe I oder im Deutschunterricht kennengelernt haben, sei hier an einem sehr kurzen Text dargestellt (bei dessen Lektüre selbstverständlich normalerweise kein *reading log* geführt wird), wie die Einführung methodisch ablaufen kann. Die Lehrerhinweise in Klammern sind als Lenkung entsprechender Eintragungen durch die Schüler beim Durchgang durch den Text zu verstehen.

Ein *reading log* sollte zwei Rubriken enthalten, die linke für den Eintrag von Textelementen, die rechte für den Respons des Lesers auf bestimmte Textpassagen.

Short short story	Reading log	
	(Elements of the text: characters, setting, key events, etc.) (Teacher: What does the title tell us? Make notes. ↓)	(Responses to the text: impressions, questions, points for discussion, etc.) (Your question ↓)
The Dying	title: sb. is dying (Teacher: Fill in the characters ↓)	but who? (Your question ↓)
1. The two policemen gazed down at him. "Is he alive ?" "His eyes are moving."	Two policemen and sb. on the ground, dying	function of the policemen? (Your comment ↓)
5. "Won't be for long." "Nope." Staccato flashes climb a distant mountain. "Poor guy."	Won't be for long! → (Teacher: What about ll. 7/8 and ll. 12/13)	macabre!
10. "What's he looking at?" "Couldn't tell you. Only he knows." A little girl skips gladly before him, dropping an infinity of flowers.	→	Discussion in class: ll. 7/8 and 12/12

3. Schülerorientierte Auseinandersetzung mit dem Text

Die in Richtlinien und Lehrplänen geforderte Selbstständigkeit und Eigenverantwortlichkeit als wesentliche Aufgabe der Sekundarstufe II lässt sich bei der Textarbeit gut verwirklichen. Das Ziel ist die eigenständige Auseinandersetzung mit dem Text, die allerdings erfahrungsgemäß einer gewissen Einübung bedarf.

Schülerorientierung erschöpft sich aber nicht im Erfragen von Eindrücken nach der Lektüre eines Textes, sondern wird nur eingelöst, wenn Schüler/innen die Auseinandersetzung mit einem Text selbst initiieren. Der Unterricht gestaltet sich so, dass in einer offenen Phase zu Beginn einer jeden Textbesprechung, von allgemeinen Schülereindrücken ausgehend, Besprechungspunkte zusammengetragen, diese zunächst ungeordnet an die Tafel geschrieben und dann mithilfe des Lehrers erweitert und in eine logische Analysestruktur gebracht werden. Die Führung eines zweispaltigen Lesetagebuches während der Lektüre längerer Texte (cf. Students' Book S. 136) ist für diese Arbeit eine wichtige Voraussetzung. Als Beispiel mag das im Unterricht entstandene *reading log* zu *Hello out there* dienen (vgl. Teachers' Book, S. 41)

Der Unterricht selbst läuft nicht in der bekannten Lehrerfrage-Schülerantwort-Kette in vorstrukturierter Form ab, die Lernenden steuern den Bearbeitungsprozess anhand des erarbeiteten Analyseschemas vielmehr so weit wie möglich selbst. Dem Lehrer fällt eine gewisse Lenkungsfunktion zu, damit das Unterrichtsgespräch in geordneten Bahnen verlaufen kann. Den Schülern wird im Appendix des Schülerbuches (S. 137ff.) für das Unterrichtsgespräch ausgewähltes Besprechungsvokabular angeboten.

4. Der Aufgabenapparat

Der Aufgabenapparat ist nicht als Leitschnur für einen lehrergesteuerten Unterricht gedacht, sondern vorwiegend für die schriftliche Nachbereitung der Unterrichtsergebnisse konzipiert; er enthält jedoch gelegentlich auch über die Textbesprechung hinausgehende Aufgaben zum problemlösenden Denken bzw. zur eigenen Meinungsbildung.

Die Aufgaben sind überwiegend gegliedert in: a) Inhalt, b) Struktur, Stil/Sprache, c) Evaluation. Das jedem Bereich zugeordnete Aufgabenbündel wird in der Randspalte in der Regel nicht mit stereotypen Überschriften (wie Awareness, Comprehension, Structure/Style, Evaluation, etc.), sondern aus motivationalen Gründen mit inhaltsorientierten Titeln versehen.

Literaturhinweise

Ken Hyland, "Purpose and strategy: Teaching extensive reading skills", in: English Teaching Forum 2/1990, S. 14ff.

George S. Murdoch, "A more integrated approach to the teaching of reading", in: English Teaching Forum 1/1986, S. 9ff.

Wolfgang Schulz, „Selbstständigkeit – Selbstbestimmung – Selbstverantwortung. Lernziele und Lehrziele in Schulen der Demokratie", in: Pädagogik 6/1990, S. 37ff.

Ian Tudor. Learner-centredness as language education. Cambridge: Cambridge University Press, 1996.

Ralf Weskamp. Fachdidaktik: Grundlagen & Konzepte. Anglistik/Amerikanistik. Berlin: Cornelsen, 2001.

Wortschatzarbeit

Theoretische Grundlegung

Wortschatzarbeit ist bisher meist noch zu stark auf das Einzelwort bezogen. Ein derartiger Zuschnitt verhindert aber eine systematische Verarbeitung des Wortguts, da beziehungslos zueinander stehende Vokabeln kein System ergeben. Systemlos betriebene Wortschatzarbeit muss unbefriedigend bleiben, weil lernpsychologisch gesehen einer isoliert angebotenen Vokabel innerhalb einer Agglomeration von Einzelwörtern jede innere und äußere Bindung an ein anderes Wort fehlt. Ein heterogener, amorpher Wortschatz dissoziiert schneller als ein assoziativ-gebündelter.

Methodische Gestaltung

Daraus ergeben sich wichtige methodische Folgerungen. Die Vokabeln dürfen nicht beziehungslos gelernt und reaktiviert werden, sie müssen assoziativ in Bezugsbündeln verankert werden, da Zusammenhängendes und Zusammengehöriges besser im Gedächtnis haftet. Sinnvoll zusammengeordnete Einzelelemente assoziieren sich und werden gemeinsam aktualisiert, wenn es darum geht, sie anzuwenden. Die assoziative Verankerung sieht die Zusammenfassung von Einzelwörtern zu Wortgruppen in Bezugsbündeln vor. Die Beachtung dieser psychologischen Wirkgesetzlichkeiten gewährleistet ein optimales Behalten im Sinne von Verfügbarhalten der Vokabeln. Von entscheidender Bedeutung bei der Systematisierung der Lexik ist die Erfassung bekannten Wortschatzes nach thematischen Gesichtspunkten.

Methodisch wird so verfahren, dass nach der Bearbeitung eines thematisch angelegten Unterrichtsabschnitts (z. B. im zweiten Kapitel des Schülerbuchs „Helpless and lonely") die innerhalb konkreter Sinnzusammenhänge in Texten und im Unterrichtsgespräch erfassten Einzelwörter aus dem Kontext gelöst und in eine neue (abstrakte) Ordnung, in sachfeld- bzw. themenbezogene Bezugsfelder gestellt werden.

Wörter werden gesammelt, sortiert und miteinander verknüpft, d. h. vernetzt und reaktiviert. Für die Vernetzung bieten sich zwei unterschiedliche Darstellungsweisen an: das *Topic Word Web* und die *Topic Word Page*. In einem *Topic Word Web* werden Assoziationswörter wie bei einer *Mind Map* oder einem *Spidergram* auf von einem Zentralbegriff ausgehenden Verästelungen notiert. Die *Topic Word Page* ist zweigeteilt und ermöglicht eine übersichtliche Anordnung von Wörtern und Wendungen. In *People Around You* erfolgt die Zusammenstellung des Vokabulars in Bezugsfeldern auf *Topic Word Pages*, weil *Word Webs* durch eine Vielzahl von Verästelungen unübersichtlich und lernunwirksam werden können und darüber hinaus meist nur Substantive erfasst werden. Bei der *Topic Word Page* werden für ein Bezugsfeld, z. B. *helplessness*, passende Wörter als sog. *headwords* in die linke Spalte, z. B. *help* und *to help*, und diesen zuzuordnende Wörter und Wendungen in die rechte Spalte geschrieben. Die innerhalb der thematisch angelegten Unterrichtseinheit in Texten aufgefundenen oder im Unterrichtsgespräch gebrauchten Einzelwörter erscheinen also in einem thematisch oder sachfeldbezogenenen Feld wieder. Die Anlage der rechten Spalte in Form von Wendungen oder *chunks* fördert die idiomatische Verwendung der Sprache.

In bestimmten Fällen bieten sich insbesondere für spätere Wiederholungen Worterklärungen in Fußnoten an.

Für die Erfassung des Vokabulars auf *Topic Word Pages* im Din-A4-Format bieten sich Sammelhefte in Form von Ringbüchern an, die übersichtlich und leicht zu ergänzen sind.

Die Anlage von Topic Word Pages sollte etwa so erfolgen:

	term	expressions	
helplessness	help	to give help	**Topic:**
	helpless	to need help	**helplessness**
	to help	(not) to be of (any) help	
	helpmate	her advice was a great help	
	helpful	helpful partner	
	without help	He came to help her.	
		to do sth. for sb.	
		to give / lend sb. a hand	

Im Anschluss an die assoziative Zusammenstellung themenbezogenen Vokabulars oder die Verwendung bereits angelegter Wortvernetzungen als Ausgangsbasis für spätere Wiederholungen bieten sich eine Reihe feldbezogener Übungen an, z. B.:

- Ergänzung von Lückentexten ohne Angabe der einzusetzenden Wörter des betreffenden Bezugsfeldes
- Bezugsfeld-gesteuerte Textproduktion nach Stichwörtern
- Mündliche/schriftliche Rekonstruktion eines mehrmals vorgelesenen Textes mit Wörtern/Wendungen des Bezugsfeldes nach Angabe von Schlüsselwörtern
- Verfassen eines Textes unter Verwendung der Wörter und/oder Wendungen des betreffenden Bezugsfeldes

Literaturhinweise

Klaus Hinz, „Wörter vernetzen und anwenden", in: PRAXIS des neusprachlichen Unterrichts 4/1999, S. 347 ff.
Herbert Holtwisch, „Mindmapping im Fremdsprachenunterricht", in: PRAXIS des neusprachlichen Unterrichts 1/1992, S. 38 ff.
Christiane Neveling, Wörterlernen mit Wörternetzen. Tübingen: Gunter Narr, 2004.
Alfred Töpfer, „Assoziative Festigung des Wortschatzes", in: Der fremdsprachliche Unterricht, 2/1967, S. 35 ff.

Prozessorientierte Schreibschulung

Grundlage für die Schulung des Schreibens sind die in den beiden letzten Jahrzehnten zusammengetragenen Ergebnisse der kognitiv orientierten Psycholinguistik über die menschliche Schreibfähigkeit und die daraus entwickelten Verfahren des Schreibens. Unter den konkurrierenden Modellen hat sich das von Hayes und Flower entwickelte Modell durchgesetzt. Das Schreiben setzt sich demnach aus drei Komponenten zusammen: dem Wissensspeicher des Schreibenden, der Aufgabenstellung und dem eigentlichen Schreibprozess. Auf die Wissenskomponente greift der Schreibende während des Schreibprozesses immer wieder zurück. Die Aufgabenstellung enthält alle Informationen, die ihm über den konkret zu produzierenden Text zur Verfügung zu stehen haben. Der Schreibprozess selbst gliedert sich in die nachstehend genannten Teilkomponenten.

Im Unterricht kommt dem Schreibprozess das Hauptaugenmerk zu. Eine Übersicht, die diesen Prozess schülernah abbildet und die auch die aus den einzelnen Stufen des Schreibprozesses abzuleitenden Einzelaufgaben enthält, sollte in den Unterricht einbezogen werden und stets Leitlinie bei der Textproduktion sein. Sie könnte wie folgt aussehen:

Board

The process of writing:	Your task:
Getting ideas together	Collect ideas and write them down using keywords.
Planning	Put your ideas in a logical order and plan your paragraphs.
Writing	Use your keywords and your plan while writing.
Revising	Check if your text concentrates on the topic and includes all important ideas and information. Improve or correct your text if necessary.

Das Schreiben ist also ein komplexer Prozess, dessen Teiloperationen durch Strategien gesteuert werden und an dessen Ende der geschriebene Text steht. Im Englischunterricht hat sich die Schreibförderung bisher weitgehend auf die Beurteilung der Schreibprodukte und auf die Begutachtung der Klassen- oder Klausurarbeiten beschränkt, d.h. die fremdsprachliche Schreibförderung ist bislang vor allem produktorientiert und beachtet zu wenig die Entwicklung von Strategien, die dem Schreiben zu Grunde liegen. Forschungsergebnisse der Psycholinguistik lehren aber, dass an die Stelle der produktorientierten Schreibförderung die prozessorientierte Förderung treten müsse. Diese beschränkt sich nicht nur auf die Formulierungsphase, sondern zerlegt den Schreibprozess in einfache Schritte mit auf diese bezogenen Aufgaben, die vom Schüler auch als Schreibtechniken eingesetzt werden können. Grundlage für ein didaktisch-methodisches Modell zur Förderung des Schreibprozesses sind die in der obigen Übersicht angegebenen Komponenten des Schreibprozesses. Sie betreffen Stoffsammlung, Gliederung der Gedanken sowie Textplanung, Schreiben und Überarbeitung.

Im Appendix des Schülerbuchs von *People Around You* wird der Übersicht halber der Schreibprozess auf zwei, jeweils zwei Teilaufgaben zusammenfassende Schritte konzentriert:

1. *Preparatory steps*, die die Stoffsammlung und die Textplanung umfassen, und
2. *Writing*, das den Schreibprozess selbst und die Überarbeitung des Schreibresultats betrifft. (vgl. Schülerbuch S. 140)

Der so zu gestaltende Schreibprozess wird beispielhaft für die im Englischunterricht der Sekundarstufe II am häufigsten gestellten Schreibaufgaben dargestellt, die im Unterricht besprochen werden und den Schülern und Schülerinnen als Leitschnur dienen sollen: Zusammenfasssung, Meinungsäußerung, Zeitungsartikel und Charakterisierung.

Literaturhinweise
Tricia Hedge, Writing. Oxford: Oxford University Press, 1988.
Klaus Hinz, Petra Schmidt, „Prozessorientierte Schulung der Textproduktion im Englischunterricht der Sekundarstufe II", in PRAXIS des neusprachlichen Unterrichts 1/1995, S. 13 ff.
Dieter Wolf, „Lerntechniken und die Förderung der zweitsprachlichen Schreibfähigkeit", in: Der fremdsprachliche Unterricht 2/1991, S. 34 ff.

Decisive moments – Short story

Funktion und Aufbau des Kapitels

Der Übergang von der Mittelstufe zur Oberstufe ist der geeignete Ort, den in weiten Teilen der S I durch die neuen Anforderungen an die Kommunikationsfähigkeiten vernachlässigten Bereich fiktiver narrativer Texte auszubauen. Dabei erscheint es wesentlich sinnvoller, dies durch die Bearbeitung einer Reihe von Short stories zu tun, anstatt ohnehin knappe Unterrichtszeit auf die Lektüre eines Langtextes zu verplanen. Die Analyse der Short story vermittelt alle Kenntnisse, die auch zur Bearbeitung eines Romans notwendig sind, und bereitet somit in Hinblick auf das Skill Training intensiver und umfassender, als dies eine Romanbesprechung leisten könnte, auf die Anforderungen im Zentralabitur vor.

Der Aufbau sowie die Textauswahl des Kapitels tragen dem Rechnung. Der Einstieg erfolgt über eines der wohl bekanntesten Pressefotos des 20. Jahrhunderts. Das Foto von Eddie Adams erfasst und verbildlicht die Bedeutung der Definition *„significant incident […] in the lives of a limited number of characters"* (Schülerbuch S. 9). Dieses Kernelement des „decisive moment" soll den Blick der Lernenden auf das gattungstypische Element schärfen.

Die Textauswahl beginnt mit einem nichtfiktionalen narrativen Text, der zum einen mit dem Kapitel 4 (*Non-fictional texts*) vernetzt, zum anderen zur Abgrenzung zum fiktionalen narrativen Text dient. Der entgegengesetzte Hemingway-Text verleugnet nicht seine Herkunft von der kurzen Pressenotiz, trägt aber gleichzeitig alle Elemente des fiktionalen narrativen Kurztextes, was diese 138 Worte kurze Geschichte ohne Zweifel zu einem der meist interpretierten Schulklassiker gemacht hat.

Die beiden anderen Texte tragen durch ihren zunehmend größeren Textumfang zum Lesetraining und propädeutisch zur Romananalyse bei. Die zwei Geschichten, erzählt aus der Sicht von Heranwachsenden, involvieren die Leser durch ihre Authentizität und die Erzählperspektive (1st person). Folgende gattungsspezifischen Merkmale und Elemente sollten den Lernenden nach der Bearbeitung der drei Geschichten bekannt sein:

- author vs. narrator
- plot/structure (exposition; rising action; climax, turning point; falling action; solution, denouement)
- theme
- point of view (1st/3rd person narrator) (limited/omniscient)
- character in a fictional text: characterisation of persons
- action (internal/external)

Literaturhinweise

Bredella, Lothar, „Literarische Texte im Fremdsprachenunterricht: Determiniertes Produkt oder ästhetisches Objekt?", in Buttjes, Dieter/Butzkamm, Wolfgang Klippel, Friederike (Hrsg.), *Neue*

Brennpunkte des Englischunterrichts (Festschrift für Helmut Heuer), Frankfurt a. M., 1992, S. 88–97

Göbel, Walter, „Kurzgeschichte", in Ahrens, Rüdiger/Bald, Wolf-Dietrich/Hüllen, Werner (Hrsg.), *Handbuch Englisch als Fremdsprache*, Berlin, 1995, S. 438–443

Haefner, Gerhard, „Rezeptionsästhetik,", in Nünning, Ansgar (Hrsg.), *Literaturwissenschaftliche Theorien, Modelle und Methoden. (Eine Einführung)*, Trier, 1995, S. 107–118

Köhring, Klaus H., „Joyce Carol Oates und die gotische Tradition in der amerikanischen Literatur," in Buttjes, Dieter/Butzkamm, Wolfgang/Klippel, Friederike (Hrsg.), *Neue Brennpunkte des Englischunterrichts (Festschrift für Helmut Heuer)*, Frankfurt a. M., 1992, S. 32–40

Nischik, Reingard M., „Teaching the American Short Story: New Approaches to an Old Favorite", in *Der Fremdsprachliche Unterricht*, 3/1999 (39), S. 28–33

Nünning, Ansgar, "But man [...] is the story-telling animal", in *Der Fremdsprachliche Unterricht*, 3/1999 (39), S. 4–13

Werlich, Egon, *Praktische Methodik des Fremdsprachenunterrichts mit authentischen Texten*, Berlin, 1986

Werlich, Egon, *Typologie der Texte*, Heidelberg, 1975

Introduction

The main intention of the introductory page is to arouse the students' attention. The photo will look familiar to a number of students. It is intended to illustrate one of the major features of a short story, the decisive moment in the lives of a very limited number of protagonists. It is closely linked to the two following texts ("Suspect Shot By Police Dies" and "Two o'clock in the morning") both of which center on violent deaths.

The photo by Eddie Adams captures the moment of death in what seems to the observer a cold-blooded deed. Adams, himself surprised by the sudden execution, later tried to correct the impression of cold demeanour, giving the circumstances of the event. The communist Vietcong prisoner had just murdered eight South Vietnamese, trying to spread terror in Saigon on this second day of the Tet Offensive (Feb. 1st, 1968). In an interview for the 1972 *AP Yearbook* Adams said:

"Sometimes a picture can be misleading because it does not tell the whole story. I don't say what he [Loan] did was right, but he was fighting a war and he was up against some pretty bad people."

The impact of this photo, the haunting expression of the victim and the discomforting reality that the executioner was an American-backed general, cannot be denied.

Possible solutions

> In task 1 students are asked to make a list of alternative actions. The range of answers will be from "questioning the Viet Cong" to "arrest/send to prison". The main focus of the discussion should be on the fact that there *are* alternatives in most decisive moments of our lives, that the decision taken at that moment marks the character of a person for life. Question 2 is meant for open discussion. The teacher should step back into the role of a listener, guiding but not interfering.

Suspect shot by police dies

Author
Bill Price comes from Georgia but has been working for WCPO-TV in Cincinnati since 1986. He is a general assignment reporter.
WCPO is a broadcast TV station affiliated with the ABC network. It belongs to the same media group as the *Cincinnati Post*. Like many German TV channels it has an internet news service, from which this text has been taken.

The report
After a chase a man is shot by police. The man tried to escape arrest after police wanted to check his car. The suspect was not armed and was driving his wife's car.

Unterrichtsempfehlungen

Der Text stellt die Verbindung zwischen nichtfiktionalen und fiktionalen narrativen Texten her. Methodisch wäre hier z. B. ein Anschluss an das Kapitel 4 denkbar. Ziel dieses ersten Textes ist, die Gemeinsamkeiten beider Textsorten herauszuarbeiten, gleichzeitig aber auch schon mögliche Unterschiede (*chronology of events*) vorzuentlasten. Der Report ist auf die Kontrastierung mit der Hemingway-Kurzgeschichte angelegt und entfaltet nur in der Zusammenschau seine ganze didaktische Wirkung. Die Textanalyse folgt dem Dreischritt von ‚*comprehension*' – ‚*analysis*' – ‚*comment*'. Hierbei wird auch die teilweise bei der schulischen Textanalyse in der S II vernachlässigte Betrachtung bedeutungstragender grammatikalischer Strukturen eingefordert (hier besonders *past tense* und *passive voice*).

Assignments – Solutions

1. Outline the main facts of the report. Start by writing a list (or a mind map) of the six "W-questions" (Who? What? When? Where? Why? How?).

> **Who**: Police (Hamilton County); Anthony Myers (42)
> **What**: a chase; suspect shot by police
> **When**: Wednesday morning
> **Where**: in Sharonville on U.S. 42
> **Why**: Myers/suspect took off; rammed two police cars
> **How**: police shot at the car; suspect killed by bullets through windshield

2. Compare the information given in the headline and the first sentence with the facts supplied in the rest of the article.

> The headline and the first sentence summarize the main facts of the report. The details are elaborated in the main part of the text.

Make a list of the words, phrases and grammatical structures which show that the author of this report was trying to give an objective representation of the event.

> **Words**: suspect; went to investigate; a criminal history; refused to elaborate
> **Phrases**: Police said (quotes); according to police; officers involved; police refused to elaborate
> **Grammatical structures**: the use of the passive voice: shot by; was closed; was shot by, was pronounced dead; were not injured

4. From your personal point of view, decide whether it was justifiable to kill Anthony Myers or not. Give reasons.

> It is obvious that the reporter presupposes that Anthony Myers was killed within the legal rules. Numerous quotes show that the police felt attacked and threatened by the suspect. The actual death of the suspect may have been an accident, the two policemen did not intentionally want to kill him, but to stop his flight. The students will nevertheless give their opinion based on German experience and will probably judge the killing as inappropriate/ overreaction, an example of "trigger-happy" police behaviour. Writing practice should focus on "give reasons". The words in the box may help students express their opinion.

At two o'clock in the morning
Ernest Hemingway

terse = kurz + bündig

Author
Ernest Hemingway (1899–1961) was born in Oak Park, Illinois. At the age of seventeen Hemingway started his career as a writer in the newspaper office of *"The Star"* in Kansas City. When the United States entered the First World War, he joined a volunteer ambulance unit in the Italian army, where he was wounded in 1918. After his return to the United States, he became a reporter for Canadian and American newspapers. At this time he developed his straightforward prose and <u>terse</u>, economial dialogue characterized by minimalism. Hemingway had a significant influence on the development of twentieth century fiction. During the twenties, Hemingway became a member of the group of expatriate Americans in Paris (The "Lost Generation"). He led a turbulent social life, and was married four times. Hemingway received the Pulitzer Prize (1953) and the Nobel Prize for Literature in 1954. In 1961, at age 61, he committed suicide.

The short (short) story
Two Hungarians have just robbed a cigar store, when two policemen arrive on the scene. They are shot by one of the policemen. As there wasn't any reason for killing the two men the second policeman questions his colleague's action. He is told off by his colleague and finally accepts his explanation.

Unterrichtsempfehlungen

Die sehr kurze Hemingway-Geschichte hat trotz ihrer oberflächlich betrachtet recht einfachen Sprache die Textdichte eines Gedichts. Der Text ist auf ein Minimum reduziert, kein Wort scheint zu viel bzw. austauschbar. Zur Unterstützung der Erarbeitung wird der Text im Schülerbuch nicht so kompakt wie in der Originalfassung abgedruckt, sondern mit Einschnitten und Absätzen, welche den Überblick erleichtern. Die Geschichte ist besonders gut zum Einstieg in die Sequenz geeignet, da sie sich von dem nicht-fiktionalen Report abgrenzen lässt und auf kleinstem Raum alle Elemente der klassischen amerikanischen Short Story vereint. In dieser extremen Verdichtung liegt natürlich auch die Schwierigkeit, ebenso in der leicht zu antizipierenden Gefahr, dass die Lernenden aufgrund ihrer Rezeptionsgewohnheiten den Moment der „Action", also die Schießerei, für den „Climax" halten. Die Aufgaben verfolgen stärker die Bewusstmachung formaler Kriterien und befriedigen vielleicht nicht die Bedürfnisse nach einer inhaltlichen Ausdeutung der Geschichte. Hier ist den Unterrichtenden nach Aufgabe 2 ein geeigneter Raum gegeben, dies, wenn als nötig erachtet, eigenständig aufzuarbeiten. Die Diskussion des „plot diagram" führt zwangsläufig zu einer Erörterung des Inhalts.

Assignments – Solutions

1. Outline the main facts of the story. Use the six "W-questions" (see also p. 8). Start by writing a list (or a mind map) of the six "W-questions" (Who? What? When? Where? Why? How?).

> **Who**: two Hungarians (burglars); two policemen (Drevitts & Boyle)
> **What**: a burglary; suspect shot by a policeman
> **When**: at two o'clock in the morning
> **Where**: at Fifteenth Street and Grand Avenue
> **Why**: Boyle shoots them because they are foreigners/'wops'.
> **How**: Boyle shoots the two Hungarians without any warning.

2. The plot diagram of a short story looks like this: Copy the plot diagram. Using line numbers (or quoting) divide the story into the parts referred to above. Be prepared to justify your ideas about the beginning and the end of the different phases.

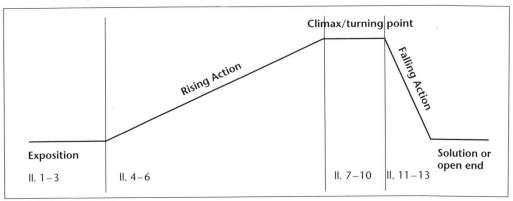

At two o'clock in the morning   19

Exposition: The first sentence is clearly exposition. The second sentence, although already giving the beginning of the rising action, might still be included, because it presents the reader with the other two protagonists.
Rising action: Lines 4 to 5 are the rising action. Line 6 may be considered as part of the climax, as it marks the opposition of Drevitts towards Boyle, but it can also be included here.
Climax: The next four lines of dialogue are the climax/turning point of this short story. One might want to include the first part of Drevitts answer ("That's all right maybe this time"), but this can also be seen as the beginning of the falling action.
Falling action: The last three lines of the story contain the falling action. Things are settled (Drevitts' worries because of their unlawful behaviour).

3. Which elements show you that this narrative is not a report in a newspaper? Make a list.

Only the first sentence might be from a report in a newspaper. The introduction of "Drevitts and Boyle" in the next sentence only implies they are policemen. The omniscient narrator can most clearly be seen in line 6 ("Drevitts got frightened…"). Students should mention the most obvious element, the dialogue passage, which isn't a quote, as in a non-fictional report. A conclusion or final sentence is completely missing.

4. Write a newspaper report about an incident like the one that the reporter Hemingway might have written for the Star.

Students may copy ideas/structures from the report (p. 8). Thus the heading might be: "Suspect shot by police"
It lies within their creative scope to accept the information given by the two police officers or to doubt the necessity of violence ("… further investigations into the use of violence/weapons are necessary…")

5. Read the news report of the highway shooting in Ohio once again and then write a short (short) story (not more than 150 words) about the incident.

As in task 4 students could begin as follows:
At two o'clock Myers was stopping his Chevrolet Blazer near some closed businesses on Conray Road. Deputy Sheriff Miller drove up in his Ford. When Myers noticed the police he got frightened and tried to get away. …
It is important that the students use the features of a short story, i.e. dialogue and a narrator.

Just along for the ride
Dennis Kurumada

Author
Dennis Kurumada was born in Salt Lake City, Utah, in 1952 as the third (of four) sons of Jun and Helen Kurumada. He wrote the short story *"Just along for the ride"* when he was a student at Skyline High School, today still, as in the 60's, an elitist school on the East Bench of Salt Lake City. The story earned him the *Scholastic Magazines' Creative Writing Award* in 1970. After graduation from high school, Dennis Kurumada studied at the Colorado College in Colorado Springs, Colorado. Today he has settled into a career as a freelance cameraman for television (covering Utah news, e.g. he shot the opening ceremonies of the 2002 Winter Olympics for International Sports Broadcasting) and movie studios (camera in "Absence of the Good," 1999, directed by John Flynn). He is married to Becky Kurumada and supports international help and human rights activities.

The short story
Five teenagers are bored and drive around in a car. During a brief discussion one of them (Phil) decides to knock someone down by opening the car door. Unfortunately their first attempt goes wrong and the car hits a boy. Not knowing whether the victim is dead or alive, they drive away panic-stricken. The first person narrator knows the boy and wants them to stop. But as another car follows them they race up into the mountains. They lose their pursuer and then drive back home. Later they learn that their victim has survived. The narrator, tormented by fear and remorse, decides to go and see the boy.

Unterrichtsempfehlungen

Die Geschichte, deren Spannungsbogen bis zur letzten Zeile anhält, sollte von den Schülerinnen und Schülern in einem Durchgang gelesen werden. Dabei kann an dieser Stelle im Rahmen des Skilltrainings das „reading log" eingeführt werden (siehe dazu die pre-reading task).
Ein möglicher Unterrichtseinstieg bietet sich über ein Cluster an, das Schüleraussagen zum ersten Bild (S. 12) aufgreift und zu ersten Vermutungen über den Text bündelt. Je nach Leistungsfähigkeit der Gruppe könnte dies eine Entlastung der Lektüre darstellen.

Board

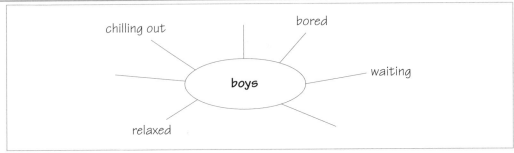

Im Anschluss an die Rezeption der Kurzgeschichte äußern sich die Schüler/innen zur Geschichte und nennen zu besprechende Gesichtspunkte, die an der Tafel in einem Diagramm festgehalten werden, z. B.

Board

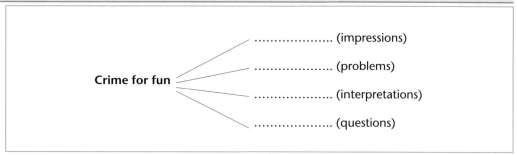

Die Betrachtung der Haltung der einzelnen Protagonisten zur Tat könnte die Besprechung des Inhalts abschließen und in einer Tabelle so oder ähnlich zusammengefasst werden.

Attitude towards the criminal act

	Phil	other boys	narrator
before the accident	wants to liven up a dull evening	unanimous approval	doubts, fear of police
after the accident	(Dick) upset by the incident (tears), fear of police, calm again after radio news		guilt ridden, inner conflict

Eine kurze Untersuchung der von den Protagonisten verwandten Sprache zur Sicherung des Verständnisses für verschiedene Sprach- und Stilebenen schließt sich nahtlos an die Analyse der Personencharakterisierung an.
Nach der Verständnissicherung (evtl. unter Einbindung der Erarbeitung eines „plot diagram") und anschließenden Aufgaben (Schülerbuch Aufg. 1 bis 3) in der Hausaufgabe oder in Partnerarbeit konzentriert sich der Unterricht auf die Erzählperspektive, die in dieser Kurzgeschichte ein Schwerpunkt der Analyse ist. Die Lernenden sollen erkennen, wie essentiell die Wahl des Erzählstandpunktes die Wahrnehmung des Lesers beeinflusst. Die unterschiedlichen Wirkungen der verschiedenen Erzählperspektiven werden durch schriftliche Aufgaben (4 und 5) vertieft. Der inhaltliche Schwerpunkt dieser Geschichte, der auf dem Gewissenskonflikt des Erzählers liegt, unterstützt den literaturdidaktischen Ansatz.
Die letzten Aufgaben (6 und 8) können ohne Vorbereitung im Unterricht bzw. als Hausaufgabe erledigt werden. Sie fördern kreative Schreibprozesse und erlauben den Schülerinnen und Schülern eine eigene Ausgestaltung (und ggf. Lösung) des Konflikts des Protagonisten bzw. eine persönliche Stellungnahme.

Decisive moments – Short story

Assignments – Solutions

1. Divide the text into five or six sections and find headings that summarise the content of these sections.

> There are several possible solutions. One possible answer is:
> l. 1 to 21   a mean plan
> l. 22 to 41   the accident
> l. 42 to 71   hit and run
> l. 72 to 86   remorse
> l. 87 to 97   no more chickening out

2. Why is the accident especially painful for the narrator?

> Students' answers should point out that he feels personally guilty and suffers an inner conflict, because he knows the victim. (You might discuss the question, whether it would be less painful if you/he didn't know the victim, and why?) At first group pressure restrains him, but after his time out he does not rejoin the group with their decision to keep quiet about the accident, but plucks up courage to take a first personal step towards atonement.

3. Describe the behaviour of the driver (Dick) after the accident? Explain his reaction (there are three different phases).

> First he is scared (l. 35) and when the narrator calls out the victim's name (Ken Benjamin) he slows down as if to stop and help the victim.
> But then he speeds away from the scene, desperate and crying (l. 45 f.).
> Finally (beginning l. 55) he regains his composure and outpaces the Volvo driver, leaving him behind in a ditch (l. 70 f.).

4. This story is told by one of the characters (we don't know his name). Try to transform the following extract (p. 13 l. 39 to l. 50) into third-person narration:

> There was a squeal of tires on the slick street and a hollow thud as the figure was hurled, rolling across the roof. *He* got all mixed up.
> "Ken Benjamin!" *he* said. "I think that was Ken Benjamin!"
> Dick slowed down. Then he suddenly started speeding down the street. "Dick! Stop! I know that guy! Dick, will ya stop?" He [Dick] didn't hear *him*.
> "Stop the car! He's my friend!"
> *He* hit him [Dick] on the shoulder and grabbed his shirt. He [Dick] turned around. Tears were blobbing up in his [Dick's] eyes.
> "Shut up, you jerk! You want us to get nailed for manslaughter?"
> He [Dick] hit *his* arm. What a stupid thing to do! *He* got so scared that *he* started shivering like crazy. *He* just couldn't believe it. *He* felt sick.

Try to describe how the different point of view changes the effect of the text on the reader.

> The main impression, apart from the loss of direct involvement (because of the different "he"), is of a more detached atmosphere. The reader is watching a dramatic scene but is no longer part of the conflict.

5. Relate the incident from the Volvo driver's point of view.

> The Volvo driver serves as the "objective eyewitness". He doesn't know any of the characters, probably doesn't even know how many are in the car. He doesn't know about the vicious plan, but has witnessed its execution. He represents the law-abiding citizen who tries to catch the culprit but heroically ends in a ditch and the villains escape. Students may add to his characterization, maybe he is a former policeman or a teacher…

6. The story has an open ending. The author has left it to the reader to imagine what happens next. Can you continue the story? Let's say Ken opens the door. Write the dialogue that might follow.

> The dialogue might start as follows:
>
> "Hi Ken!" I said. "Glad to see you're ok."
> "What do you mean. How do you know about the accident?"
> "Well, I was in the car.…"
>
> Students should convey the feeling of guiltiness and remorse. The narrator might take a detached view of what happened. Does he try to excuse the deed, to explain what happened? There are several possibilities but the solutions should fit the character readers met in the text.

7. Make a list of all slang expressions/teenage language in the story. What is the intended effect on the reader?

> […] gonna be a total loss (l. 3)
> […] things have gotta be pretty dull (l. 3f.)
> Man, … (l. 7)
> […] knock the guy on his can. (l. 13f.)
> […] kinda funny. (l. 15)
> Whenever we wanna have some fun, you always chicken out. (l. 20f.)
> I kinda hoped (l. 65)
> We were out in the sticks by now. (l. 67)
>
> The use of slang expressions and teenage language serves to characterise the narrator and the atmosphere of the story. These expressions are especially frequent in the first few paragraphs of the story, later on there are only a few examples. They are intended to give the story an authentic flavour.

8. Could the person telling the story have prevented the accident?

> The answer is open and depends on the students' judgement. The list of useful expressions permits a negative as well as a positive answer to this question. Different opinions should be compared and discussed.

Small avalanches
Joyce Carol Oates

Author
Joyce Carol Oates is one of the most highly regarded north American writers of our time. Born on June 16, 1938, in Lockport, New York she has never lost her attachment to rural America throughout her work. After school she studied at Syracuse University and graduated as valedictorian in 1960. Just a year later Oates received an MA in English from the University of Wisconsin.
Already in 1959 she earned her first award, the *"Mademoiselle college fiction award"*, for her story *"In the Old World"*. Her life followed an unspectacular path, being often called a "workaholic" writer, she continued both her academic and literary careers at the same time. In 1965 she married Raymond J. Smith and later the couple settled in Detroit, Michigan, where she taught English Literature at the University of Detroit. In 1968 they crossed the border to live in Canada for the next 10 years, where Oates taught English Literature at the University of Windsor (Canada). In 1978 she became a member of the American Academy of Arts and Letters. Since 1978, Oates and Smith, who as a couple also publish *The Ontario Review*, have lived in Princeton, New Jersey, where she first worked as writer in residence and later became a professor in the creative writing program.
Her writing has earned her much praise and many awards, including the Rosenthal Award (1968) for *"A Garden of Earthly Delights"*, the National Book Award (1970) for *"them"*, and the PEN/Malamud Award for Excellence in Short Fiction (1996).
To date (2006) she has published 50 novels and novellas, 29 short story collections, eight books of poetry, eight drama collections, 11 non-fiction volumes, 17 anthologies, six books for children and young adults, as well as hundreds of uncollected stories, poems, articles, essays, and reviews.
Her style has been described as "weaving an emotional thread", and that is exactly what happens in *"Small Avalanches"*. The reader is slowly drawn into the story, following the path of the protagonist (Nancy, a 13 year old girl). Though some of Oates' stories are marked by violence this story totally lacks external aggression, but at the same time conveys a strong feeling of fear, oppression and victimization. The reader might, at first sight, tend to stereotype the seemingly superficial teenage narrator, but will soon find that these stereotypes are what makes the aggressor (the man) tick, but do not depict the girl's character. The story seems to be timeless. First published in the eighties it has recently been republished in a collection of short stories (for young adults), bearing its name as a title.

The short story

An attractive teenage girl (Nancy, 13) is followed by a man on her way home. Obviously the man is trying to approach her, although he does not show his real (paedophile) intentions. The girl, followed by the man on her shortcut up a hill, escapes and leaves him behind, apparently suffering a minor heart attack from chasing after her, and goes home.

Unterrichtsempfehlungen

Diese recht lange Kurzgeschichte (5018 Wörter) eignet sich zum propädeutischen Lesetraining im Hinblick auf fiktionale Langtexte. Die Geschichte zerfällt (im Text im Schülerbuch optisch markiert) in zwei Teile, wobei der erste Teil sehr handlungsarm ist und hauptsächlich zur, für eine Kurzgeschichte ungewöhnlich detaillierten, Figurencharakterisierung der Erzählerin dient. Die Ereignislosigkeit und die damit aufkommende Langeweile wird dem Leser überzeugend vermittelt und könnte bei Schülerinnen und Schülern, die noch keine großen Leseerfahrungen haben, zu Motivationsverlust führen. Gleichwohl ist dieser Teil für das Verständnis des Verhaltens der Hauptperson unverzichtbar. Das Mädchen sehnt sich offenkundig nach einer gleichwie gearteten Abwechslung und Unterbrechung ihres eintönigen Lebens. Die Gefahr, die dann von dem fremden Mann, der sie auf ihrem Heimweg verfolgt, ausgeht, wird von ihr daher nur sukzessive erahnt, während der Leser sie schnell viel stärker spürt.

Die Pre-reading Activities sind auf die Unterstützung dieses Aspekts ausgelegt und helfen damit den Lernenden in den für sie ungewohnten Handlungsort des Midwest der USA hineinzufinden. Der Kartenausschnitt (S. 16) kann im Unterrichtsgespräch durch eine Amerikakarte ergänzt werden, auf der die Lernenden den Staat Colorado suchen. Dies könnte durch Bildmaterial veranschaulicht werden, wobei bevorzugt die Weite und Leere des Raumes betont werden sollte. Die Schülerinnen und Schüler könnten Mutmaßungen anstellen, warum die Straßen so gradlinig verlaufen. Die Impulsfrage „What might be one of your main problems?" kann zu einem Cluster, oder, bei ordnendem Anschrieb, zu einer Mindmap ausgestaltet werden.

Board

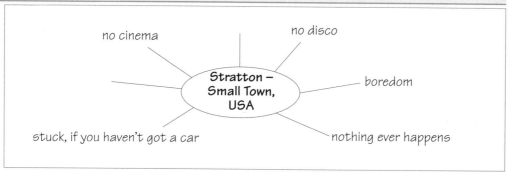

Der erste Teil der Geschichte kann zum Training des extensiven Lesens verwendet werden. Sinnvoll ist hier der Einsatz des Tonträgers, der, beim gleichzeitigen Mitlesen, eine zügige Rezeption ermöglicht. Im Anschluss daran sollten die das Mädchen betreffenden Fakten in ein paar Sätzen zusammengetragen werden. Auch der zweite Teil könnte bei der Erstbegegnung vom Tonträger unterstützt werden; hier ist es danach aber sinnvoll, den Text gründlich zu bearbeiten (intensives Lesen), um z. B. die spannungserzeugenden Elemente herauszuarbeiten. In der Randspalte der Kurzgeschichte finden sich einige While-reading Aufgaben, die besonders in der intensiven Lesephase die Aufmerksamkeit der Lernenden auf bestimmte Skills (Nachschlagen von Wortbedeutungen und Bedeutungsvarianten sowie Hilfestellungen zum *note taking*) lenken.

Letztlich sollte darauf hingewiesen werden, dass die Geschichte von Mädchen häufig anders rezipiert wird als von ihren Mitschülern. Die Erfahrung hat gezeigt, dass Jungen z. T. den bedrohlichen Aspekt der Handlungen des Mannes nicht erspüren, während die Schülerinnen sich gut in Nancys Situation hineinversetzen können, eine solche oder ähnliche Angstsituation auch z. T. schon erfahren haben. Hier sollte im Unterrichtsgespräch sensibel gearbeitet werden, um eine mögliche Betroffenheit angemessen einfließen zu lassen.

Assignments – Solutions

1. Retell the story in five sentences.

> A teenage girl (Nancy) is bored and spends the afternoon at her uncle's garage until a man drives up to the gas station and talks to the uncle.
> When Nancy walks back home, the man follows her and talks to her.
> Nancy tries to get rid of him and takes a shortcut through the fields and over a hill.
> The man runs after her and tries to catch her, but on his way up the hill he falls down and seems to suffer from a heart attack.
> Nancy leaves the man and walks back home.

2. Why do you think the man follows the girl?

> There is no valid proof that the man wants to harm the girl. He might be just a friendly man, a bit bored on his trip through Kansas, a man who enjoys talking to young people. Nevertheless some of his questions and allusions may lead to a different interpretation. Here are some examples:
>
> "So your house must be way back there?" l. 286; "I like shortcuts and secret paths", l. 297; "[…] all sorts of little traps and tricks for me, huh?" l. 325; "Hey. That's against the rules." l. 330; "Little Nancy, you're like a wild colt or a deer, you're so graceful – is this your own private secret path? Or do other people use it?" ll. 334–337; It was like a game. "Come on, Nancy, slow down, just slow down," he said. "Come on, Nancy…", ll. 356f.; "This is a little trial for me, isn't it?" he said. "A little preliminary contest. Is that how the game goes? Is that your game, Nancy?", ll. 367f. and finally: […] He said something that sounded like, "won't be laughing –" but I couldn't hear the rest of it. […] l. 379f.
>
> The notion of the secret path, the idea of a game that they are playing does not fit in with his too friendly attitude and hints at other, evil intentions. The expressions offer a choice of these different interpretations, though the idea that he is a paedophile, following a young teenage girl should be emphasized in discussion. Attention should be paid to the frequent use of "embarrassed" as well as Nancy's feeling that something "[…] felt strange" (e. g. in line 186f.).

3. In which parts of the story do we have mainly external action and where is internal action predominant? Use the line numbers for your findings.

> In the first part internal action is predominant (l. 1 to l. 20). This is followed by a short dialogue section, that might be classified as external action (l. 21 to l. 49). The following paragraphs are confined to internal action (l. 50 to l. 94), followed by another dialogue exchange (l. 95 to l. 124). The next few lines down to l. 142 are mainly internal action, interrupted by 3 lines of dialogue. With the arrival of the man external action becomes dominant, though lines 163 to 171 are mainly internal once more. The following pages are dominated by external action and the first longer section of internal action begins at line 414. The last part (l. 430 to l. 445) is marked by the dialogue between mother and daughter (external action).

4. Look again at line 249 to 421. Draw a graph showing the speed of movement (go >; walking fast >>; run >>> etc.) and the change of altitude (up ↗ – down ↘). Refer to the list you made earlier (words and actions of the man and the girl).

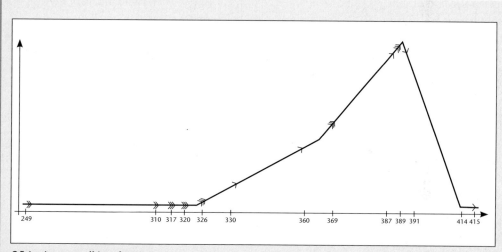

Line	Action
254	I was walking fast
310	[I] started to walk faster
317	I began to run a few steps
320	I kept running
326	I ran up the side of the hill
338	I was walking backward up the hill
360	a big rock higher up and I went around
369	I ran higher up the hill, off to the side where it was steeper
387	I just stood there grinning
389	[I] ran up the rest of the hill, going almost straight up the last part
391	right on top I paused
414	I walked over to the other side
415	[I] went along the path to our lane

5. Draw a plot diagram (see also p. 10). Compare it with your graph from task 4.

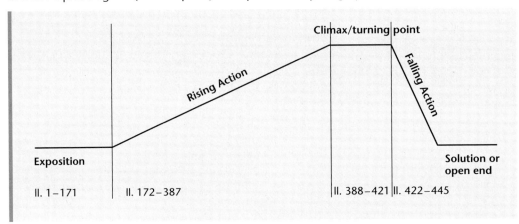

Students could be asked to present their graphs on overhead transparencies. The similarity between the two graphs should be evident. The only difference is in the first part of the rising action, where the chase at first is along a level path before it goes uphill.
When Nancy reaches the top of the hill this is also the climax and turning point of the story.

6. In pairs discuss whether you think this short story would be more interesting, if you left out the first part, up to the moment when the man arrives in his car (l. 143).

Students might have different opinions here, though the characterisation of the first person narrator in this part, which becomes an important factor later on, should be discussed in class. The generally accepted notion that in a short story nothing is superfluous, should be made clear.

7. Draw a mind map of the characters in this short story.

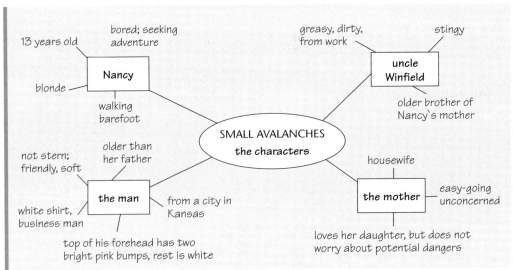

8. Try to find a picture (in a magazine/newspaper, etc.) of a girl that resembles the narrator. Discuss your choice. Use your mind map to support your choice. Whose picture comes closest to the girl in the story? Take a vote.

> This tasks helps to reactivate (and complete) the vocabulary for characterisation. The main features of the girl are given in the mind map, so students should come up with attractive (curly) blonde teenage girls, casually, even untidily dressed for hot weather.

9. Now do the same for the man.

> Nancy's description of the man is not so clear; first she says he is about the age of her father (l. 235), then she says he looks older (l. 268). He is "shorter" than her father (l. 267). His outward appearance and social status should be that of a businessman, with a friendly smile, but something malignant behind his face. The "two bumps" (l. 340) on his forehead, "pink, sunburned" may give him a devilish appearance. The photos should be used for extensive discussion (link to task 2 is possible). He should be slightly overweight and look unfit.

10. What is the theme of this short story? Give reasons.

> The theme of the story is, generally speaking, "Growing up". The teenage girl is lured into a dangerous situation, of which she is not completely aware. Male aggression/paedophiles are also part of the theme of this story, though never as a dominant or explicit aspect.

11. Do you think the girl (Nancy) is to blame for what happened?

> The discussion will be very open. Male students may view the situation differently from female. Counsellors would point out that Nancy doesn't say NO clearly enough right at the beginning. She gives in to his "game", flattered (??), because she feels that he sees the woman in the young girl. General agreement should be reached that teenage girls should be able to walk the streets barefoot and in shorts without being sexually harassed.

Thematic vocabulary: boredom – violence – responsibility

	term	expressions	
responsibility	responsible someone's duty obligation	to take responsibility for doing sth. to accept full responsibility for sth. to claim responsibility for sth. to bear the responsibility to be somebody's fault to be on someone's conscience to be accountable for sth.	**Topic:** **boredom – violence – responsibility**

Klausurvorschlag

I used to live here once
Jean Rhys

She was standing by the river looking at the stepping stones and remembering each one. There was the round unsteady stone, the pointed one, the flat one in the middle – the safe stone where you could stand and look round. The next wasn't so safe for when the river was full the water flowed over it and even when it showed dry it was slippery. But after that it was easy and soon she was standing on the other side. The road was much wider than it used to be but the work had been done carelessly. The felled trees had not been cleared away and the bushes looked trampled. Yet it was the same road and she walked along feeling extraordinarily happy. It was a fine day, a blue day. The only thing was that the sky had a glassy look that she didn't remember. That was the only word she could think of. Glassy. She turned the corner, saw that what had been the old pavé had been taken up, and there too the road was much wider, but it had the same unfinished look.

She came to the worn stone steps that led up to the house and her heart began to beat. The screw pine was gone, so was the mock summer house called the ajoupa, but the clove tree was still there and at the top of the steps the rough lawn stretched away, just as she remembered it. She stopped and looked towards the house that had been added to and painted white. It was strange to see a car standing in front of it.

There were two children under the big mango tree, a boy and a little girl, and she waved to them and called "Hello" but they didn't answer her or turn their heads. Very fair children, as Europeans born in the West Indies so often are: as if the white blood is asserting itself against all odds.

The grass was yellow in the hot sunlight as she walked towards them. When she was quite close she called again, shyly: "Hello." Then, "I used to live her once," she said. Still they didn't answer. When she said for the third time "Hello" she was quite near them. Her arms went out instinctively with the longing to touch them.

It was the boy who turned. His grey eyes looked straight into hers. His expression didn't change. He said: "Hasn't it gone cold all of a sudden. D'you notice? Let's go in." "Yes let's," said the girl.

Her arms fell to her sides as she watched them running across the grass to the house. That was the first time she knew. (449 words)

Assignments
1. Describe the situation of the girl/young woman.
2. Illustrate the author's use of grammatical structures to contrast the situations "once" and "now".
3. Imagine you are the girl/young woman. Write a diary entry and evaluate your new experience of being different.

Solutions

1. A (coloured) girl (or young woman, the text gives no clear indication of her age, but she can be considered an adolescent or even a young woman) comes back to the home of her childhood. At first the way is familiar and she remembers how it was in her youth. But then she notices changes, that have, from her point of view, damaged the landscape. Her feeling of coming back home is affected by these changes. Then she sees the house and the two white children playing in front of it. This brings back old memories and so she approaches the two children in an open and friendly way. She is shocked, when the boy suggests that he and the girl should go back inside the house and so refuses any, even verbal, contact.

2. Students should point out the use of the passive, often combined with the past perfect (work had been done carelessly; trees had not been cleared away; pavé had been taken up; screw pine was gone; house that had been added to and painted white) to illustrate the change between the past situation and the present.

3. Students should base their argument on the results of Task 2, but write personally, as if they were the girl/young woman. It is obvious that not only the landscape has changed, but also her status at her old home. They might use knowledge from other parts of the book (i.e., p. 33, the way you use the word "Hello") to underline their evaluation.

Documentary photographs
Jerzy Kosinski (1975)

While organizing my prints and negatives, I set aside several files for documentary photographs. I often carry a small automatic camera and a couple of extra rolls of film in my pocket. If I happen upon an accident, collision, fire or shoot-out, I snap as many shots as possible and later arrange them into a complete photographic reconstruction of the incident.

Recently I saw a young woman slip while crossing the street, falling directly in the path of an oncoming taxi. Just as she slipped, she screamed, and I raised my camera, getting photos of the entire incident. Her shoulder and neck smashed against the front fender, which dragged her five or six feet. I rushed over to her. While other bystanders tried to comfort her, I began taking pictures from every side. I wanted to establish on film the precise angle and position of the wheels at the moment of collision, the distance that the woman's body was dragged and the exact nature of the cab's contact with the body. By the time the police and ambulance arrived, I had used three rolls of film. When I told the taxi driver that I had photographed the accident, he said he was anxious to have the prints for his defense. He gave me his name and address, and I promised to contact him. Next, I told the police I had photos of the collision and was eager for the woman's family to see them in case they decided to sue. I was immediately supplied with the name and address of the woman, who at that moment was lifted into an ambulance.

In my apartment, I developed the negatives and enlarged some of the photographs. I selected shots for the cab driver that could best prove his innocence: according to his set, the woman had crossed the street in the middle of the block and tripped because of her high heels. The street surface had been wet, slippery and slightly inclined, and the traces made by the cab's sudden braking indicated it had stayed within its lane.

The woman's set of photos, which I mailed to her relatives, suggested she had been hit by a careless driver who hadn't noticed her crossing. It looked as if she had waited on her side of the dividing line for the cab to pass, and had fallen only after its fender had knocked her off balance.

(406 words)

Helpless and lonely – Drama

Funktion und Aufbau des Kapitels

Das Drama als wichtiges, in den Unterricht der Sekundarstufe II einzubeziehendes Genre wird in *People Around You* in zwei überschaubaren Kurzformen vorgestellt, da die Arbeit mit Kurzdramen auf den Umgang mit längeren dramatischen Formen vorbereiten kann. Am Beispiel des Kurzdramas wird der Schüler sozusagen in nuce mit dramatischen Bauformen und Darstellungsmitteln bekannt gemacht und erhält Einsichten in Wesen und Struktur dramatischer Sprache.

Kurzdramen konzentrieren sich auf punktuelle Situationen und auf entscheidende Momente im Leben von Menschen. Zu den durch die Kürze bedingten Merkmalen dieser Literaturform gehört die Konzentration auf wenige wesentliche Elemente:

- Einheit von Ort und Zeit,
- geringe Zahl der Figuren,
- Beschränkung auf die Darstellung wesentlicher Charakterzüge der Personen,
- keine Nebenhandlung,
- unmittelbare Hinführung zur Problematik in Grenz- und Krisensituationen,
- wendepunktartige Aufgipfelung,
- knappe und rasche Lösung des Konflikts.

Für das Drama allgemein gelten folgende gattungsspezifische Eigenschaften, die den Schülern und Schülerinnen bei der Bearbeitung der beiden Texte bewusst gemacht werden sollten:

- Im Drama fehlt (mit Ausnahme des epischen Theaters) eine Erzählinstanz, die vermittelnd und deutend in den Geschehensablauf eingreift.
- Die dargestellten Figuren konfrontieren den Rezipienten unmittelbar; sie stellen sich als Redende selbst dar und konstituieren damit die Situation.
- Die Darstellung erfolgt als permanente Gegenwart, selbst wenn Vergangenes dargestellt wird. Das in der Epik vorhandene Spannungsverhältnis von erzählter Zeit und Erzählzeit ist weitgehend aufgehoben.
- Die Sprache (Dialog) erfüllt vielfältige Funktionen: sie erklärt die Charaktere, veranschaulicht die Problemsphäre, treibt die Handlung voran und kann außerdem Atmosphäre und *setting* konstituieren.
- Der Dramentext besteht aus dem Haupttext (*dialogue*) und dem Nebentext (*introduction* und *stage directions*). Die Bühnenanweisungen sind integraler Bestandteil des Textes und erlangen dadurch große Bedeutung, insbesondere bei der Verwendung des Dramas als Lesetext. Sie sind nichtverbale Ausdruckselemente, die sich auf die Verhaltensweisen der Schauspieler oder auf die Bühnengestaltung beziehen. Aus diesem Grund sind die Schüler anzuhalten, sie bei der Interpretation nicht aus dem Auge zu verlieren.

Das literaturdidaktische Ziel dieses Kapitels ist demnach darin zu sehen, den Schülerinnen und Schülern anhand des hier vorgestellten *playlet* und *short play* die wesentlichen, oben genannten Charakteristika eines dramatischen Textes nahezubringen. Insbesondere sollte die Unterscheidung von Haupt- und Nebentext (*main text* und *supporting text*) und deren Funktion für den Handlungsverlauf herausgearbeitet werden.

Obwohl ein Kurzdrama im Allgemeinen dialogisch gestaltet und meist handlungsarm ist, bietet es sich für die Interaktion zwischen Leser und Text an, Erwartungshaltungen zum Inhalt des Textes nicht nur in der *pre-reading*-Phase aufzubauen, sondern auch durch in den Text eingestreute Fragen und Beobachtungsaufgaben zum weiteren Fortgang des Geschehens (vgl. *Hello out there*, S. 38 ff.).

Das Kapitel mit seinen zwei dramatischen Kurztexten ist so angelegt, dass das kurze *playlet* mit seinem Aufgabenapparat sozusagen dramenpropädeutischen Charakter trägt und die Funktion der Hinführung zu einem längeren dramatischen Text, dem *short play*, erfüllt. In ihm steht schon allein wegen seines einfachen Gehalts nicht die Inhaltsanalyse im Vordergrund, sondern die Erarbeitung wesentlicher dramentypischer Charakteristika, nämlich der konstitutiven Elemente eines dramatischen Textes und der dramentypischen Mittel der Figurenzeichnung.

Literaturhinweise

Klaus Hinz, „Das Kurzdrama im Englischunterricht", in: PRAXIS des neusprachlichen Unterrichts 2/1987, S. 127 ff.

Heinz Kosok, „Das moderne englische Kurzdrama", in: Neusprachliche Mitteilungen aus Wissenschaft und Praxis 2/1970, S. 131 ff.

Berthold Schik, „Das Kurzdrama im Fremdsprachenunterricht', in: Der fremdsprachliche Unterricht 1/1979, S. 16 ff.

Introduction

The aim of the pre-reading activities on the introductory page is to arouse students' interest in reading the plays by helping them to anticipate the beginning or the content of the playlet and the short play.

The students are asked to speculate about the situation at the start of each play and to make notes on the options from the expressions "Hello, there" and "Hello out there".

Possible solution:

Hello, there!
Sb. greets somebody on his walk.	(Héllo↗ – pause – there↘)
Sb. wants help from a person some distance away.	(Héllo, thére↗)
Sb. greets somebody as he wants to have a word with him.	(Héllo thére↘)

Hello out there!
Somebody calls for help from a locked car.	(Héllo – pause – out thére↘)
Somebody calls out from his cell.	(Héllo – óut thére↗)
Somebody calls for help from a burning house.	(Héllo↗ óut thére↘)

Vocab result
"Hello" is used
a) when meeting or greeting somebody,
b) to attract somebody's attention.

"Hello out there" is used
a) to address somebody who can be seen outside a room.
b) to call somebody who cannot be seen, e.g. from a closed room.

A helping hand
A playlet by Stephen Speight

Author
Dr. Stephen Speight, M.A (Oxon). Comprehensive school teacher for five years, lecturer in English at a College of Education for three years. Senior lecturer at the University of Dortmund for 30 years. Co-author of "Good English", "Let's go" and "Britain: Get ready for the trip". Author of numerous readers for learners of English, "Right or Wrong" (a guide to correct usage), "English Newspapers and Television", "The Fascination and Risks of Technology" and "The different Faces of Britain".

The play
A young man is jogging out in the countryside when he happens to see an old lady who is trying to change a wheel on her caravan. He offers to help. As the wheel nuts are very rusty it takes him some time to change the wheel. When he suggests that the lady should ring the Automobile Association for help next time she replies that she has not got a mobile phone. The young man offers to help her choose a good one at the phone shop in town later in the morning, but the lady does not turn up at the agreed time.

Unterrichtsempfehlungen

Die Bearbeitung des playlet beginnt mit dem Aufgreifen der entsprechenden pre-reading-Aufgabe auf der Einstiegsseite und kann anschließend nach dem *lehrergestützten* „student centred approach" in drei Schritten erfolgen:

1. Auditive Präsentation mit anschließender offener Phase und Inhaltsanalyse
2. Vergleich von Hör- und Drucktext
3. Personencharakterisierung anhand des Drucktextes

1. Auditive Präsentation, offene Phase und Inhaltsanalyse

Das *playlet* sollte über Tonträger präsentiert werden. Alternativ kann die Präsentation auch durch darstellendes Lesen mit verteilten Rollen erfolgen, was angesichts des einfachen Inhalts ohne vorherige Analyse gerechtfertigt ist. Allerdings ist sicherzustellen, dass die beiden ausgewählten Kursteilnehmer (ein Mädchen und ein Junge) den Text evtl. mithilfe des Lehrers gründlich studieren und den Vortrag nach dem *Read and Look up*-Verfahren unter Einbezug von Hintergrundgeräuschen vorher einüben.

Vor der Darbietung des *playlet* sollten folgende Vokabeln erklärt werden:
drunken lout, puncture, jack, to undo wheel nuts, spanner, a piece of pipe

In der recht kurzen *offenen Phase* sind etwa folgende Schülerbeiträge zu erwarten:
"an easy but nice play", "it's nice to see the old lady showing some initiative", etc. (allg. Eindrücke)
sowie
"young man", "lady": *main characters* (Inhalt).

Der Inhalt des auditiv präsentierten *playlet* wird nicht lehrergesteuert zusammengetragen, sondern lerngruppengesteuert durch selbstständige Beiträge der Schüler/innen erschlossen. Je nach Verlauf des Gesprächs kann die erste Aufgabe des Aufgabenapparats bei der häuslichen Nacharbeit entfallen. Die genannten Aspekte können anschließend in wenigen Sätzen zusammengefasst oder in eine Tabelle (Strukturierungshilfe durch den Lehrer) als Ausgangspunkt für die spätere Charakterisierung der beiden Personen eingetragen werden. Die Tabelle kann entsprechend den Schülerbeiträgen etwa so gefüllt werden:

Board: Structured analysis of the content

young man	lady
meets old lady	who has a puncture
changes wheel on lady's caravan (using spanner/piece of pipe)	not very practical/strong unable to change wheel
offers to help lady choose a mobile phone, makes arrangement and keeps it	does not keep the appointment

2. Hör- und Drucktext: Ein Vergleich

Nachdem das playlet individuell gelesen worden ist, müssen die beiden Textformvarianten „main text" (Haupttext) und „supporting text" (Nebentext) unter Einbezug der Infobox (Schülerbuch, S. 35) im Plenum erarbeitet werden.

Die wesentlichsten, von den Schülern genannten Unterscheidungsmerkmale zwischen Hör- und Drucktext werden gesammelt und in ein vom Lehrer entworfenes Raster eingetragen. Beispiel:

Board: Listening to plays – reading plays: a comparison

Spoken play (radio play)	Printed Text	
Main text	Main text (Haupttext)	{ dialogue { monologue
Supporting text missing (unnecessary: characters speak, noises can be heard – but no hints for the stage)	supporting text (Nebentext)	{ introductory { remarks { stage directions
The play on stage	Printed text only the script for the production	
Lively three-dimensional impression		

3. Personencharakterisierung anhand der Druckvorlage

Die Personencharakterisierung wird durch die Besprechung des Info-Kastens (Schülerbuch, S. 36) vorbereitet. Es empfiehlt sich, einen auf Folie geschriebenen Raster zu projizieren und im Plenum Beispiele für jede der vier Charakterisierungsformen zu sammeln und einzutragen oder im Sinne einer stärkeren Schüleraktivierung die Aufgabe in Kleingruppen erledigen zu lassen. Dazu muss das nachstehende Arbeitsblatt für jede Gruppe kopiert werden. Das Verfassen des Charakterisierungstextes erfolgt später in der Hausarbeit.

Worksheet

	lady	man
main text		
directly		
indirectly		
supporting text		
directly		
indirectly		

Die dritte Aufgabe des Aufgabenapparats braucht nicht im Unterricht vorbereitet bzw. behandelt zu werden, sondern kann ganz der individuellen Hausarbeit vorbehalten bleiben. Das Gleiche gilt für die vierte schüleraktivierende/handlungsorientierte Schreib- und Dialogisierungsaufgabe.

Assignments – Solutions

1. How does the young man help the lady?

> The young man offers to change a wheel for the lady on her motor caravan. He rummages around in her toolbox and tries and uses different tools to undo a very rusty wheel nut. Later he is prepared to help the old lady choose a mobile phone in a phone shop, but he waits for her in vain at the agreed time.

2. Find examples for direct and indirect forms of characterisation … and characterise the two people in a few sentences.

a) Direct and indirect forms of characterisation

	man	lady
Main text		
directly	helpful (l. 9)	helpless (ll. 14 ff.), not very practical (l. 17), enjoys trips (ll. 21 f.), feels lonely (ll. 16 f.).
indirectly	practical (ll. 35 f., skilled (ll. 31 ff.)	left (mechanical) things to her husband (l. 18)
Supporting text		
directly	young (l. 1), a student (l. 28), smart tracksuit (l. 2), new trainers (l. 2) long and floppy hair (ll. 2 f.)	old (l. 4), white hair (l. 4), steel-rimmed glasses (l. 5), baggy and faded tracksuit (ll. 5 f.)
indirectly	skilled (ll. 33 f.), reliable (ll. 53 f.), patient (ll. 53 f.)	possibly unreliable (l. 54)

b) Preparing the characterisation in a chart,

outward appearance	abilities/character	behaviour and actions
man	**man**	**man**
young student, about 20 smart tracksuit, new trainers hair: rather long and floppy	helpful practical skilled strong	changes wheel patient does not give up when there are difficulties
lady	**lady**	**lady**
old, a widow white hair steel-rimmed glasses baggy and faded tracksuit	unskilled not very strong/practical unreliable (?)	feeling lonely, enjoys travelling around and likes camping

c) Characterisation

The characters in the playlet are a young man and an elderly lady.
The 20 year old man, a student who lives nearby, seems to be a keen jogger. He wears a smart tracksuit and almost new trainers. His hair is rather long and floppy, typical of young people. The lady, a widow, is rather old, her hair is already white and she wears steel-

rimmed glasses. Since her husband died she feels rather lonely. But she enjoys travelling around in her small motor caravan and probably likes camping. She also wears a tracksuit, but hers is baggy and faded which shows that she must be either poor or careless about her clothes.

The student is very helpful and practical. He manages to undo a rusty wheelnut for the lady so that the wheel with the puncture can be changed. The lady is not very practical, she cannot change a wheel on her caravan and is also unable to operate a mobile phone.

3. Turn the beginning of the playlet into a narrative text (up to l. 18). Which version do you think is more effective?

A young man was jogging out in the countryside when he happened to see an old lady who was trying to change a wheel on her small motor caravan.

He asked the lady if he could lend her a hand. The lady told him that she had stopped by the gate for lunch where she had run over a broken bottle probably thrown there by a drunken lout. When the young man asked her about her problem she told him that she had a puncture and was changing a wheel; she had been able to undo three wheel nuts but the fourth one would not move. If her husband, who was very good with mechanical things, had still been alive she would not have had a problem like this.

The playlet is much more dramatic than the narrative version. Even though the play is not performed on stage we have the feeling that we are experiencing the events described.

4. How about writing another scene that shows how the playlet could go on?

Ideas for the open task:
- Old lady explains why she is late. They go into the shop together.
- Old lady explains why she did not come, she has already been in the shop and bought a mobile phone for herself, she wanted to assert her independence.
- Old lady excuses herself for being late; she got lost in town.
- etc.

Hello out there!
A short play by W. S. Saroyan

Author
William Stonehill Saroyan was born in Fresno, California, on August 31, 1908, the fourth child of Armenian immigrants; he died on May 18, 1991 of prostate cancer at the age of 72. Saroyan wanted his heart to be buried in the Armenian highlands. A year after his death, half of his cremated remains were permanently enshrined in the Pantheon of Greats in Yerevan, Armenia, while the other half remained in Fresno, California.

William Saroyan was an internationally renowned Armenian-American writer, playwright and humanitarian. His fame and his most enduring achievements as a writer date from the 1930s. He entertained millions with hundreds of short stories, plays, novels, memoirs and essays which continue to charm and touch us today. Among Saroyan's best short plays are *My heart's in the Highlands* (1939) and the curtain-raising *Hello out there* (1942) which was first performed in New York in the same year. *Hello out there* is less often read and more often performed, particularly in college one-act festivals.

In 1953, Jack Beeson wrote a libretto *Hello out there* in one act adapted from Saroyan's play. The world premiere of the chamber opera was on May 27, 1954 in New York directed by Felix Brentano and conducted by William Rhodes.

The play
A young man is imprisoned in a small-town jail for an alleged rape. He calls out from his cell hoping to make contact with someone outside. He is answered by a young girl who works in the prison as a cook. As they talk their mutual loneliness brings them closer together. The young man, a drifter and a gambler, paints a picture of their possible life together in freedom in San Francisco. The girl, with some hesitation, accepts his love and his dreams. They both find comfort in this new relationship. However, before she can help him to escape, their dreams are shattered by the intervention of the husband of the allegedly raped woman. Preferring lynch-justice to reason, the husband kills the young man. Any hopes the young couple had of breaking out of the world they are both 'imprisoned' in, are shattered by irrational violence.

Unterrichtsempfehlungen

„Hello out there!" ist sprachlich und inhaltlich leicht zugänglich und eignet sich besonders für die Erstbegegnung mit einem Kurzdrama. Die Kürze des Textes erlaubt die vollständige individuelle Lektüre in häuslicher Vorbereitung, wobei die Schüler/innen wie bereits beim playlet mit ihrer Lösung der pre-reading-Aufgabe die Lektüre des Dramas beginnen und sehen, ob ihre Inhaltsprognose zutrifft oder ob Modifikationen vorzunehmen sind.

Die folgende Unterrichtsbeschreibung ist als Anregung für den eigenen Unterricht zu verstehen, bedeutet also nicht, dass dies der einzige methodische Weg ist, da verschiedene Faktoren einen modifizierten Unterrichtsverlauf und andere Unterrichtsergebnisse bedingen können. Die hier vorgestellte Besprechung des Dramas umfasst die offene Phase, die Inhaltsbesprechung und die Erörterung gattungsspezifischer Aspekte.

Offene Phase:
Die erste Stunde wird mit einer offenen Phase eingeleitet, in der die Schüler/innen ihre Eindrücke artikulieren und Besprechungspunkte nennen können. Nach vorausgegangener häuslicher Lektüre des Dramas leidet naturgemäß die Spontaneität im Unterricht. Es muss daher stets Teil der Hausaufgabe sein, persönliche Eindrücke und Reaktionen auf bestimmte Ereignisse während des Lesevorgangs in einem Lesetagebuch (*reading log*, vgl. Students' Book, p. 136) niederzuschreiben, so dass diese während der offenen Phase im Plenum geäußert und festgehalten werden können. Falls in einem Kurs die Führung eines „reading log" noch nicht eingeübt worden ist, muss dies vor der Lektüre des Dramas anhand des kurzen Beispieltextes (Teachers' Book, S. 8) erfolgen.

Möglicher Lesetagebucheintrag:

Elements of the text (characters, setting, key events, etc.)	Response to the text (impressions, questions, comments, points for discussion)
young man in prison cell, calling *Hello out there*, ll. 7f.	why in prison?
girl (prison cook) answers, l. 11	
reason for imprisonment: accused of rape. People from Wheeling will come and break in, ll. 219f.	loneliness: point for discussion
girl (Katey) also lonely, l. 63	
young man flatters her, ll. 47f.	exaggerated
wants to marry her, l. 95	unreal and incredible
gradual development of relationship, ll. 72–95	should be discussed in class
hope for a better life with her in S. Francisco, l. 259, ll. 380ff.	plan: nonsense
young man asks her to help him break out, ll. 296ff.	difficulties husband's behaviour should be discussed
While Katey is getting her father's gun the woman's husband appears and kills him Katey finds him lying on the floor: dead	interpretation of the end in class

Beispiel eines „spider diagram" für Leseeindrücke

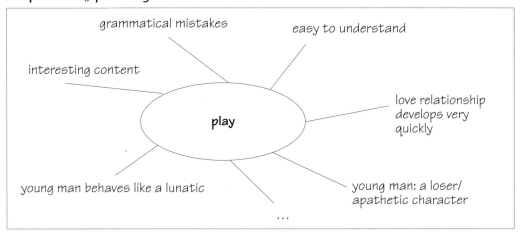

In die offene Phase fließen nicht nur die während des Lesens entstandenen Eindrücke ein, sondern auch die Aspekte, die die Schüler/rinnen in die Besprechung des Textes einbezogen wissen wollen. Ein Schüler sammelt diese nach Nennung zunächst ungeordnet an der Tafel; Erweiterung und Ordnung können ggf. mithilfe des Lehrers erfolgen. Das Analyseschema steuert später das Schülergespräch.

Board: Impressions and aspects of analysis (ein Beispiel)

Tafelanschrieb (ungeordnet)	Tafelanschrieb (erweitert und geordnet)
situation at the beginning	situation at the beginning
the girl's future	call: Hello out there
husband a villain?	content of the play
character of the wife	loneliness
helplessness	helplessness
structure of the play	love relationship
love relationship	husband of the allegedly raped woman
theme of the play	(kills young man)
loneliness	end of love relationship
meaning of the repeated call "Hello – out there!"	theme of the play
	structure of the play
	language in the play
	function of the supporting text

Analyse des Dramas

Die Analyse des Kurzdramas, bei der die von den Schülern/innen vorgetragenen Besprechungspunkte aufgegriffen werden, betrifft Inhalt und gattungstypische Merkmale.

1. Inhaltsanalyse

Die Handlung eines Kurzdramas konstituiert sich nicht als logisch verknüpfte Folge verschiedener Ereignisse. Das Strukturmerkmal des Kurzdramas ist vielmehr das Umkreisen einer bestimmten, von Anfang feststehenden Situation, die verdichtete Darstellung einer ausschnitthaften, zufälligen Szene mit offenem Ausgang. Das Geschehen in *Hello Out There* in seiner ganzen Dimension zu erfassen, ist daher das Anliegen der Eingangsbesprechung.

Die von den Schülern in der offenen Phase für die Inhaltsbesprechung genannten Punkte werden aufgegriffen, jedoch von der Lehrkraft möglichst in ein literaturdidaktisch stringentes Schema gebracht:

Board

Content → – (a) surface structure (Oberflächenstruktur: grobe Inhaltserfassung)
– (b) deep structure (Tiefenstruktur: tiefere Bedeutung inhaltlicher Fakten)
↓
✦ Helplessness and loneliness of the young man
✦ Establishing a love relationship

Die Schüler führen die Untersuchung der einzelnen Punkte bzw. Teilthemen selbstständig durch und belegen in der Zusammenfassung ihre Ergebnisse mit Beispielen aus dem Text, der Lehrer greift nur lenkend ein.

a) Oberflächenstruktur (Surface structure)
Die Oberflächenstruktur des Inhalts kann in einigen Sätzen zusammengefasst oder im Tafelbild stichwortartig je nach Schülerbeiträgen etwa so festgehalten werden:

Board: Content of the play

young man	girl
– imprisoned for an alleged rape	– answers
– calls out from his cell to make contact with someone outside	– accepts and shares his dreams
– paints a picture of a new life together in freedom	– is willing to help him escape from the prison

husband (of the allegedly raped woman)
destroys their plans by killing the young man

b) Tiefenstruktur (Deep strucure)
Die Erschließung der Tiefenstruktur in der Krisensituation umfasst zwei Gesichtspunkte, die sich getrennt besprechen lassen, thematisch jedoch ineinandergreifen: Hilflosigkeit und Einsamkeit des jungen Mannes sowie Entwicklung der Beziehung zwischen den beiden jungen Menschen.

- Hilflosigkeit und Einsamkeit des jungen Mannes
  Das Leben des jungen Mannes verläuft glücklos und lässt ihn in tiefer Einsamkeit zurück. Glücklos irrt er von Ort zu Ort umher, bleibt aber einsam und hilflos. Diese Hilflosigkeit setzt sich im Drama fort, als er völlig verlassen aus seiner Gefängniszelle heraus durch Hilferufe Kontakt zu irgend jemand außerhalb der Zelle zu finden versucht. Schließlich knüpft er Kontakte zu der jungen Köchin, die ihn aus seiner Hilflosigkeit befreien will.
- Entwicklung der Beziehung zwischen den beiden jungen Menschen
  Der junge Mann versucht aus seiner Einsamkeit heraus mit den Worten *Hello out there* Kontakt zur Außenwelt zu finden. Sein Rufen wird von Emily, der jungen Köchin des Gefängnisses, beantwortet. Es entwickelt sich, bedingt durch die beiderseitige Einsamkeit, rasch ein Liebesverhältnis. Das Zusammentreffen mit Emily weckt bei dem jungen Mann die Hoffnung auf eine zufriedene Zukunft. Er plant, sie zu heiraten und gemeinsam mit ihr in San Francisco ein neues Leben zu beginnen. Der Höhepunkt ihrer Zuneigung ist mit einer gegenseitigen Liebesbeteuerung erreicht. Dem sich anbahnenden Glück wird jedoch ein jähes Ende gesetzt, als der Ehemann der angeblich vergewaltigten Frau erscheint und den jungen Mann tötet.

Die Schüler untersuchen beide Aspekte in arbeitsteiliger Gruppenarbeit

(Gruppe 1: Helplessness and loneliness of the young man
Gruppe 2: Establishing a love relationship)

und notieren ihre Ergebnisse für die anschließende Vorstellung im Plenum.
Es ist damit zu rechnen, dass etwa folgende Punkte zusammengetragen werden:

Helpless and lonely – Drama

Gruppe 1 (Helplessness and loneliness of the young man)
- lonesome as a coyote all his life
- unfortunate: a gambler, wandering from town to town, hoping for luck will change
- now desperately lonely in a prison cell
- calls out to the outside world
- wish to establish contact with somebody
- contact with the young cook
- cry for help

Gruppe 2 (Establishing a love relationship)
- meeting Emily enables the young man to plan a new future
- tells her how pretty she is, girl is touched by his flattery
- takes her hand and kisses her
- decides to marry her and take her to San Francisco
- persuades her to help him break out of the prison
- the two people in love:
- girl: "Nobody anywhere loves anybody as much as I love you".
  man: "Hearing you say that, a man could die and still be ahead of the game".
  end of love relationship

2. Gattungstypische Merkmale

Im zweiten, jedoch kürzeren Teil der Unterrichtseinheit werden zwei gattungstypische Merkmale in den Blickpunkt gerückt, die bei der Behandlung des *playlet* nur kurz angesprochen worden sind und hier vertieft werden: Funktion des Nebentextes und Polyfunktionalität dramatischer Sprache.

Function of the supporting text
Bei der schulischen Beschäftigung mit dramatischen Texten, wo Dramen lesend rezipiert werden, tragen die außersprachlichen Textsegmente (*supporting texts*) in Form von *introductory remarks* und *stage directions* zum Verständnis des Textes entscheidend bei. Dies kann im Unterricht anhand des in das Kurzdrama einführenden Textes und des ersten Textausschnitts mit Bühnenanweisungen gezeigt werden.
Mögliches Ergebnis der Analyse, die der Lehrer steuert:

a) **Introductory remarks** (ll. 1–6) (instead of an exposition)	**Function** explaining the situation at the beginning of the play
	Young man: – in a prison cell, – taps on the floor with a spoon, – gets up and begins walking around, – stops at the center (centre) of the cell, – doesn't move for a long time, – feels his head as if it were wounded, – looks around and calls out dramatically

b) **Stage directions** (ll. 7–10) (instead of a description in dialogue form)	**Function** describing the two people's situation or distinctive characteristics
pause/long pause	The pauses intensify the impression of the young man's loneliness and hopelessness, especially because there is no response to his calls.
dramatically	expresses his desperation
comically	points to the impact the repeated call of the same words will have on the reader or audience
voice sweet, soft	describe the girl's attractiveness

Function of the language in dramatic texts
Sprache ist im Drama zwar nicht alleiniges Ausdrucksmittel, sie ist jedoch ein wichtiger Träger der Aussage und sollte daher an dieser Stelle kurz besprochen werden. Sprache charakterisiert in verdichteter Form Figuren, weist auf schichtenspezifische Differenzierungen hin, stellt die Reaktionen der Personen auf ihre Umwelt dar, verdeutlicht Beziehungen zwischen den Figuren und entwickelt aus dialogischen Konflikten Handlung. Die Polyfunktionalität der dramatischen Sprache lässt sich mit folgenden Funktionen transparent machen:

- Appellfunktion (Beeinflussung des Gesprächspartners),
- expressive Ausdrucksfunktion (Selbstcharakterisierung),
- referentielle Darstellungsfunktion (Darstellung der Verhältnisse aus eigener Sicht).

Im Unterricht kann so verfahren werden, dass die folgenden drei sprachlichen Äußerungen aus „Hello out there!" an die Tafel geschrieben und ohne Verwendung von Fachtermini auf ihre Funktion befragt werden.

Examples

Listen, Katey. Do what I tell you. Go get that gun and come back.	I am a gambler. I don't work. I've got to have luck, or I'm a bum. I haven't had any decent luck in years.	He's a liar.
Function (Solution) ↑ telling people what to do, influencing people	↑ self-characterisation	↑ expressing opinions

Anschließend können die Schüler/innen in Partnerarbeit weitere Äußerungen für die einzelnen Funktionen sammeln und diese in die entsprechenden Spalten eintragen.

Assignments – Solutions

Die Aufgaben im Schülerbuch greifen einige im Unterricht behandelte Probleme auf, sie sind jedoch so angelegt, dass die Schüler/innen teilweise aus anderer Perspektive eigenständig Texte verfassen müssen. Die meisten Aufgaben erfordern dagegen eine weitergehende, selbstständige Beschäftigung mit dem Dramentext.

An informal talk in class

> See: "Unterrichtsempfehlungen, offene Phase"

1. Describe the situation at the beginning of the play.

> At the beginning of the play a young man in a small-town prison cell is tapping on the floor with a spoon. It sounds as if he is trying to tap out a message. After a while he feels his head, as if it were wounded, looks round his lonely cell, and then calls out in a challenging voice: "Hello – out there!" At first no one answers, but after several more calls the voice of a young girl answers him.

2. Why has the young man been imprisoned?

> The young man has been imprisoned for allegedly raping a woman in a small town called Wheeling. He had gone into a lunch bar and sat down at the counter. A woman had come in, had sat down next to him and then started talking to him about a record that was being played. They left the restaurant together and walked a short distance before coming to the woman's home. She invited him in. He accepted, thinking that she, like himself, was lonely. Once inside, however, she demanded money from the young man, which he refused. She warned him that she would make trouble if he did not give her some money. When he continued to refuse, she ran out of the house screaming that she had been raped. Shortly after, the husband of the screaming woman returned and knocked the young man unconscious. For his own safety he was taken to the prison in Matador, a small town about seventeen miles from Wheeling.

3. Why does the husband shoot the young man?

> The husband shoots the young man because he wants to "save face". His original intentions were to save his wife's and his own reputation, by taking the law into his own hands and "punishing" the alleged rapist in the crude ways of the old American South. When he hears the young man's story he knows that his claim to be protecting his wife's honour is just a sham. However, he cannot admit this, either to himself, or in front of his companions. Therefore, to prevent the story of his own and his wife's shame being told in public, he panics and shoots the young man.

4. What do the young people have in common?

> The main thing that the young people have in common is loneliness. Both of them say that they are "as lonesome as a coyote". The young man is a rootless drifter, wandering from town to town hoping for some luck. The girl is trapped in the small town where she was born, in a dead-end job, with nothing to do but listen to "the lonesome wind lifting the dirt and blowing out to the prairie". Although their backgrounds are different, their lives are equally empty. The young man dislikes the idea of work (it is both the hard and the easy way) and hopes to make his money gambling on horses, but he is dogged by bad luck. The girl feels equally unfortunate. Her parents would not let her leave the town, and her father takes her meagre wages. The boys of the town all laugh at her. Both of them feel that life is unkind, and both are desperately looking for affection.

5. Describe the beginning, climax and end of their relationship and then put the main points in a graph.

> The relationship starts with him hearing her voice and saying, "I can tell from your voice you're O.K." Moved by her compassion he tells her how pretty she is, despite the fact that we, the readers, and she herself, know she is not. She is, however, touched by his flattery and moved when he tells her that she is sweet and he is going to marry her. She even lets him call her Katey. When she offers to run two miles to the drugstore and buy him a packet of cigarettes with the money she has saved, he takes her hand and kisses her. He is genuinely concerned about her future. She runs off, but returns a few seconds later, afraid to leave him in case something happens. He tries to calm her down and gives her money to go to San Francisco. His belief in her makes her finally say: "Nobody anywhere loves anybody as much as I love you". At this point the climax of their relationship is reached, and the young man replies: "Hearing you say that, a man could die and still be ahead of the game." The play ends with the violent and irrational shooting of the young man by the husband. The young man has just time to tell the girl to get away from the small-town small-mindedness which has led to his death, and that he will always be with her. His death puts an end to their short-lived dreams of happiness together.
>
>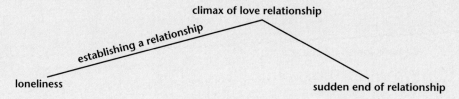

6. Which key words indicate the young people's situation and the theme of the play?

> The theme of the play is the loneliness and misfortune of people who, either because of the lack of opportunity or through their own inadequacies, find themselves at the bottom of the social pile. If we look at the number of times certain words occur which have to do with misfortune, fear, loneliness, and also the (probably misguided) hope of escape/happiness e.g. money and San Francisco, we see that these words underline the theme of the play.

48   Helpless and lonely – Drama

The words
lonesome/lonely/alone occur	15 times
scared	11
jail	7
luck/bad luck	9
money	14
hello out there (contact)	15
hello out there (cry for help)	8
San Francisco/Frisco	16
Somebody/anybody/nobody	26

7. Examine the level of language employed in the play and find out what class of society the young people belong to.

The level of language can be judged by the lexical items and the grammatical structures. It is not only what the characters say, but how they say it, that indicates the class of society to which they belong. The language used is informal. The short forms of the verb are frequent don't, I've, you're, etc., and the sentences are short and simple. The colloquial American usage of 'go + infinitive without to' also occurs, e.g. *you go tell your father*. In addition to the informality of the language, many substandard forms occur, both in vocabulary and structure. In the following list there are elements of slang, double negatives, incomplete verb forms and personal pronouns instead of demonstrative pronouns.

> We'll highroll the hell out of here
> I' aint
> you're a dog
> I'm kind of lonesome
> I been trying to think
> Who you calling now?
> How come I don't get no jello?
> study up
> I'm scared them fools are going to

From these examples we can see that the young couple belong to a not very well-educated lower class.

8. How are the words "Hello out there" used to structure the play?

The play begins and ends with the words "Hello out there". These words keep recurring throughout the play. The play is not divided into scenes, but the words "Hello out there" help to give the play a certain structure by changing the emphasis of the meaning of the words in the play.
Firstly, at the beginning of the play the words are used by the young man to establish contact with the outside world. When the girl's voice answers him and asks him why he keeps saying that, he answers "I'm lonesome".
Secondly, when the girl has appeared and they have exchanged a few words he repeats the

words "Hello out there". When the girl asks who he is calling now he replies "you". He repeats the words again and the girl answers, "Hello". This time the call is more personal and the girl's answer consolidates the relationship.

Thirdly, the words are used as a cry for help. The young man is angry at the way the girl's father treats her, and angry at the world. He wants to escape. His cry is partly a cry of defiance and partly for help.

Lastly, the words are used by the girl after the death of the young man. Her hopes have been disappointed, and she is alone. Now it is she who whispers "Hello out there!" She whispers to the outside world – to us – not expecting to be heard. The play has come full circle.

words "Hello out there" = structure of the play

| wish to to establish contact with with sb. | call for human contact | cry for help | Emily's cry to the outside world |

9. What is your opinion of the way Saroyan describes and handles the young man's situation? Open question. The following ideas can be expected:

- Saroyan does not give a detailed description of the young man's situation at the beginning but in the course of the play,
- arouses tension,
- young man's sudden affection and deep feelings for Emily unrealistic,
- his plans hardly workable/practicable.

10. Is the husband more of a villain or a victim in this play?

The husband is trapped in the same small-town environment as the two protagonists. He, however, has a reputation to keep up – a reputation based on the myth (once strongly adhered to in the South) that women, especially one's own wife, must be "pure and faithful". When he discovers that his wife is nothing better than a prostitute, he feels that his world is crumbling around him. He does not shoot out of any evil desire for brutality or violence, but in a vain attempt to defend himself from the truth, which is too painful to bear. In this play there are no straightforward villains and no real heroes. Both the young man and the girl were prepared, at least in theory, to shoot their way out of their problems. If there is a villain, it is perhaps the environment in which they are all imprisoned, and from which none of them really knows how to escape.

Would you like to learn something about Saroyan's life and works? Do some research on the Internet.
The following Internet addresses can be visited:
http://www.kirjasto.sci.fi/saroyan.htm
http://www.cilicia.com/armo22_william_saroyan.html
http://www.armenianhouse.org/saroyan/saroyan-en.html

50 Helpless and lonely – Drama

Thematic vocabulary: helplessness – loneliness

	term	expressions	
loneliness		a lonely traveller/place to live all alone alone in one's life without a companion to avoid company	**Topic:** **helplessness – loneliness**
helplessness	helpless	utterly helpless unable to act without help unhelpful not helpful helpless old lady/baby helpless with laughter	
help	help	to give help to need help to be of (any) help her advice was a great help to accept help	
	to help	he came to help her to do sth. for sb. to give/lend sb. a hand	

Zum Klausurvorschlag S. 51

Wenn die ca. 3 Wochen umfassende Unterrichtseinheit „Drama" durch weitere Kurzdramen oder ein mehraktiges Drama erweitert wird, bietet sich die nachfolgende Klausur zur Leistungskontrolle an.

Die *Assignments* sind dreigeteilt: die ersten drei Aufgaben beziehen sich auf den Bereich *Comprehension*, Aufgabe vier auf die Struktur, und Aufgabe fünf trägt textevaluierenden Charakter.

Zum Additional text S. 54

Der Zusatztext enthält keine Annotationen und keinen Aufgabenapparat. Er soll den Schüler/innen die Möglichkeit bieten, einen Dramenauszug selbstständig und eigenverantwortlich zu bearbeiten, nachdem sie in diesem Kapitel Verfahren der Analyse und Interpretation dramatischer Texte kennen gelernt haben.

Martha and Karen

A dramatic scene by Roger Karshner

Characters:
MARTHA and KAREN

In this scene between Martha and Karen, sisters, attention is focused upon profound effects of paternal indifference.

MARTHA: Father never loved anybody but himself. The unfeeling bastard.
KAREN: Do you think he loved Jane?
MARTHA: I doubt it. But we'll never know. Jane took that secret to her grave.
KAREN: They always seemed so happy.
MARTHA: Maybe he was. But with him it was for appearances. A sham. His whole life was a sham.
KAREN: It was hard to tell about Daddy.
MARTHA: No it wasn't, not really, not when you spent time with him. He was transparent. I could see right into him.
KAREN: You were closer to him than anybody.
MARTHA: Unfortunately.
KAREN: He trusted you. He took you into his confidence. You were the only one who knew about the business.
MARTHA: I was his confidant in his corrupt little game.
KAREN: The way he flaunted Jane. And so soon after Mother's death.
MARTHA: That was for shock value. That's the way he operated.
KAREN: Do you miss him?
MARTHA: No! I'm glad he's dead.
KAREN: Martha!
MARTHA: It's true.
KAREN: I miss him.
MARTHA: That's because you didn't really know him. You never saw him grind people and make them feel small.
KAREN: No, but I sensed it in him.
MARTHA: He destroyed Joe. He used him and made him promises and set him up. His signature was on all the papers and when the investigation came down Joe got the blame for everything. And Father didn't turn a hand. Joe may have committed suicide but Father killed him just as though he'd put a gun to his head.
KAREN: Why couldn't he love us?
MARTHA: He wasn't capable.
KAREN: And it cost us.

---

sham sth. that is not what sb. pretends that it is (lt. ALD)

confidant a trusted person
to flaunt to show sth./sb. in order to gain the admiration of other people

MARTHA: Yes, and I hate him for it. For not giving us even an ounce of feelings. He ruined me. I'm just like him.

KAREN: You're not.

MARTHA: I am. No warmth because I never ever got any. I'm as cold as Daddy. The same. He made sure of it. He handed it down by example. He made sure I'd keep the tradition. He wanted me to hate him. It was his plan; for me to feel nothing and be cold and hard and calculating and indifferent. I haven't felt anything for anybody else since I was a child. I'm an iceberg. I may smile and appear to be concerned but there's nothing behind it. Damn! I wonder what it's like to be able to feel, to be able to love.

KAREN: I'm sorry.

MARTHA: Help me, Karen.

KAREN: You give me warmth, Martha.

MARTHA: No.

KAREN: Yes, yes you do. And you're not like him. You may think you are, but there's a difference. You care about people.

MARTHA: Never.

KAREN: About the employees. Look what you've done for them.

MARTHA: Nothing.

KAREN: That's not true.

MARTHA: Anything I've done is out of selfishness; for the sake of efficiency.

KAREN: No. That's a lie you're trying to sell yourself. You may try to gloss over feelings but they're there. You can't take it out of your eyes. You were stuck with a thankless job and you've done wonders with it because you care. Yes, alright, you're tough. Thank God. Better tough like you than soft like me. You stepped in after Father died and took hold and made things work. You held the family together. Hell, you saved the community! And you have friends whether you know it or not. If it wasn't for you half the men in this city would be on the streets looking for work. Yes, you have a lot of Daddy in you alright. But there's a difference. The difference is that at the heart of you, deep down where it counts… you're good.

to gloss over sth.
to treat/see sth. in a superficial way

Assignments

1. Name the people mentioned in "Martha and Karen" and add a few remarks on their role in the dramatic scene.
2. What are Father's relations with his daughters?
3. How do Martha and Karen differ from each other as far as their relations with their father are concerned?
4. How does the writer keep the reader in suspense?
5. Explain why the introduction is a correct reference to the text.

Solutions

1. Key words: Martha and Karen: sisters – Mother: dead – Father: dead, was a business man, flaunted Jane (also dead) shortly after Mother's death – Joe: one of Father's employees

2. The father did not have any feelings for Martha and Karen, his paternal care was rather indifferent. Martha was Father's confidant in his corrupt business. But he did not love either her or Karen – did not give either of them an ounce of feeling (l. 35). He was not able to feel, to love (ll. 32f.). And, what is even worse, he wanted to hand his behaviour down by example. Martha should "keep the tradition […], feel nothing and be cold and hard and calculating and indifferent" (ll. 39f.).

3. The father was unable to love his daughters, to feel anything for them. But probably Martha was the one who had to bear more unhappiness than her sister. That's why she does not miss him whereas Karen does. And that's why the consequences of missing care and love are quite different. Martha feels that her father has moulded her and that she is absolutely like him: "I haven't felt anything for anybody else since I was a child" (l. 42). She is not happy and quite helpless. Karen tries to help when she reassures her "Yes, you have a lot of Daddy in you, alright. But there's a difference. The difference is that at the heart of you, deep down where it counts … you're good". (l. 67)

4. Although there is no action in the scene, the writer keeps the reader who is interested in Father's paternal indifference in suspense. In the talk between Martha and Karen, Karshner portrays Father's social manners in detail. He starts with Martha's statement "Father never loved anybody but himself". This fact is elaborated in the scene, first by mentioning his relations with Jane, whom he met shortly after his wife's death, but whom he never really loved; his life was a pure sham (l. 8).
Karshner keeps the reader in suspense by inserting a short description of the way Father treated Joe, one of his employees.

5. The introduction refers directly to the main points in the text: effects of paternal indifference. Key words: Father unconcerned about education – did not love his daughters, gave them no warmth. – Consequences: Father moulded Martha, who is unable to feel anything for other people ("cold as an iceberg"), hates her father and does not miss him.

The split decision (excerpt)

A short play by William Moseley

Characters:
DAVID: in his twenties
GINGER: in her twenties

In the words of the playwright "David is a one-dimensional, insensitive bore – which would make us wonder why a woman like Ginger would ever hook up with him to begin with".

The action takes place in an apartment in a Midwestern university town in the present time.

SETTING. The living room of Ginger and David's apartment. One half of the room is hers. Its low, comfortable sofa, framed needlework and macramé wall hanging, soft drapes, and throw rugs give it a warm, home-like atmosphere. The other half of the room is his. More like a lab than a home, its steel desk with a home computer, its tile floor without carpets, its chrome and plastic furniture, and modern, abstract graphics on the walls create an effect of cold practicality und efficiency.

AT RISE: Lights up on DAVID, seated at his desk, facing the audience, typing at the keyboard of his computer. After a few moments, GINGER enters, carrying a serving tray with coffee pot, cups, saucers, and spoons. She stops unhappily when she sees DAVID working. Then she crosses to set the tray on the coffee table in front of the couch.

DAVID: (hearing the dishes rattle, but not looking up) Ginger –?
GINGER: (only half serious) Know what, David? Some evening you're going to be all absorbed in that machine, and call out "Ginger?" – and it won't be me.
DAVID: (barely listening, continuing to work.) Hmm? And who'll it be?
GINGER: Oh … maybe nobody.
DAVID: Yeah, well – Have to put this in memory, so I can boot it up for Harris tomorrow morning.
GINGER: You gave me a full report – all through dinner. While I was hoping we'd have time to talk about –
DAVID: (interrupting) I'm nearly finished – final details on that conversion job for the city libraries. Gotta get the data from their card catalog system into MARC Records. Harris generates these broad concepts, then can't see the trees for the forest. Me, though – I'm good with –
GINGER: (overlapping) "Good with details"… (as she sits on sofa.) So you've said in detail ever since you got home from work. I'd been hoping we could talk about our –
DAVID: (continuing, over her.) Harris depends on me – to blaze a trail through his forests. Nobody on the committee ever thinks I might be smart enough to invent a marketable concept. (finishing, he turns off computer and pushes his chair back, as Ginger begins pouring coffee.)

GINGER: I made the kind you like – we got the beans in fresh at the shop today. (She holds out cup on saucer to him. He rises and crosses to take cup, leaving her holding saucer. She shrugs and sets it back down.)

DAVID: (sipping coffee, musing.) "Concept" – that's all I need. (turns away, lost in thought) Something really different – creative …

GINGER: (She hesitates, then tries.) I – now and then I get ideas. If it's a new idea you need, I might … I could help – (But he cuts her off with a scornful look and a derisive "Ha!" Rebuked, she goes on after a couple of beats.) Anyway … I thought you like the detail work.

DAVID: I do … usually. You can get lost in it, though – get lost in the trees. You keep asking yourself when you'll raise a forest of your own. (sinking onto sofa.) Now walking into a committee meeting with an original project proposal – software to sell hardware – well, it'd make me feel – feel more real, I guess. It'd prove something …

GINGER: (after a moment, tentatively) Maybe – maybe if you stopped thinking about it for a while –

DAVID: Now Ginger, I don't need more of your donut-shop philosophy –

GINGER: No, listen. Lots of university people come into the shop, right? And they say that when a person has a problem to solve, best thing is to switch your mind to some other problem, totally unrelated, and –

DAVID: Yeah, yeah – and suddenly your subconscious comes up with a solution to your first problem. The "eureka" process.

GINGER: The –?

DAVID: (condescending) "You – – reek – – ah." Greek.

GINGER: Oh. Whatever. All I know is, one of the professors will be sitting at the counter, dunking a Krispy-Kreme and bitching about his car's transmission – when all at once he'll jump up, yell "I got it!" – and go running straight out the door … no check, no tip, no nothing. (a beat) That's why I tell the girls to always collect from university people in advance.

DAVID: My transmission is fine … I don't have another problem to kick around, while my subconscious comes up with an original program to sell.

GINGER: Yes, you do. You have another problem. (a beat) We have another problem. (short pause. David sighs and pushes himself to his feet.)

DAVID: (moving to his side of the room.) But it's a closed system, dammit, whenever we try to discuss it! We go through scene after scene, nothing conclusive, around and around like – like –

GINGER: Around and around like – a donut? (David snorts a "Ha!" but she goes on.) A donut … that's what it's turning into, this – this non-marriage of ours.

DAVID: "Non-marriage" –?

GINGER: They used to call it "shacking up" – I like "nonmarriage" better. Or would you prefer "trial marriage"? But how many trials run for five years, David? (a beat – no response from him) All right, how about "living together"? – that's pretty non-committal. Or maybe "free-style relationship"? with your "spouse equivalent"?

DAVID: Ginger, come off it –

GINGER: "Relationship," then. After five years, my spouse equivalent, this "relationship" of ours is turning into a donut.

DAVID: (dropping into a chair at his desh.) Damn I hate it when you're frivolous!

GINGER: You're always saying I don't have imagination. (rising) But this afternoon, making a – a – – special donut for a lady – it, really did cross my mind that our living together's getting more and more like a donut. (crossing to him) A comfortable shape that's soft and light enough – sweet, too, on the outside. But it gets a little sticky if you hold onto it too tight, or for too long a time –

DAVID: (turning away) And I hate it when you're so illogical –

All you need is love – Poetry

Funktion und Aufbau des Kapitels

Das vorliegende Kapitel soll die Schülerinnen und Schüler in die Arbeit mit der literarischen Gattung *Poetry* einführen. Erfahrungsgemäß sperren sich Schülerinnen und Schüler zunächst gegen die Auseinandersetzung mit den vermeintlich schwer verständlichen kurzen Texten. Daher steht am Beginn der Arbeit eine thematische Heranführung an das Thema Liebe durch die Beschäftigung mit zwei aufeinanderzurasenden Herzen. Die produktive Schreibaufgabe, in Partnerarbeit einen Dialog der beiden zu verfassen, stimmt die Schülerinnen und Schüler auf das Thema Liebesgedichte ein. Auch die nächste Aufgabe, ein Gedicht in Prosa umzuschreiben, zeigt, dass man keine Angst vor Gedichten zu haben braucht.

Da es unwahrscheinlich ist, dass man mit allen Schülerinnen und Schülern alle Gedichte lesen kann, ist das Kapitel in einen obligatorischen und einen fakultativen Teil eingeteilt. Nach der Lektüre des Pflichtteils sollten die Schülerinnen und Schüler eine große Anzahl von Fachbegriffen in das *cluster*, das sie aufgrund der Anregung auf S. 61 im Schülerband angefertigt haben, eingetragen haben. Eine Zusammenfassung wichtiger Fachbegriffe findet sich am Ende des Kapitels im Schülerband auf den Seiten 76/77.

Im ersten Teil findet man als einführende Texte das Gedicht *Central Park at dusk*, das von den Schülerinnen und Schülern in Prosa umgeschrieben werden soll. Danach folgt ein Klassiker, Marlowes *The Passionate Shepherd to his love*, der mit der Idealisierung der ländlichen Idylle bekannt macht. Im Gegensatz dazu steht das moderne, im *free verse* verfasste *Comeclose and Sleepnow* von Roger McGough.

Die nächsten drei Gedichte (*Serious luv*, *First love* und *O when I was*) beschreiben in unterschiedlicher Ernsthaftigkeit die Gefühle, die man bei der ersten Liebeserfahrung hat. Dagegen beschreiben die nächsten Gedichte *Ending*, *40-Love* und *Poor girl* das Ende von Beziehungen aus unterschiedlichen Gründen. Die Texte *To my son*, *For Heidi with blue hair* und *For a good dog* zeigen die Liebe zu Familienmitgliedern und Haustieren.

Daneben gibt es Anregungen, die Schülerinnen und Schüler selbst poetische Texte verfassen zu lassen. Dies erfolgt sowohl bei der Besprechung von *Shape* und *Acrostic poems* als auch bei dem Text *To my son*, für den eine weitere Strophe verfasst werden soll.

Im Verlauf der Arbeit an den Gedichten sollen die Schülerinnen und Schüler befähigt werden, selbstständig lyrische Texte inhaltlich zu entschlüsseln und zu erkennen, mit welchen sprachlichen Mitteln Dichter Bilder erzeugen. Aufgrund dieser Fähigkeiten sollen sie in die Lage versetzt werden, selbstständig Gedichte zu analysieren und zu beurteilen, ob ein Gedicht gelungen ist oder nicht.

Literaturhinweise

Ronald Carter, Michael N. Long. The Web of Words. Cambridge, Cambridge University Press, 1987
Der Fremdsprachliche Unterricht, Mai 1987 (Themenheft: Lieder und Gedichte)
Fry, Stephen, The Ode less Travelled, London, 2005
Klarer, Mario, An Introduction to Literary Studies, London/New York 2004
Nünning, Vera und Ansgar, Grundkurs anglistisch-amerikanische Literaturwissenschaft, Klett, 2004

Introduction

Der Einstieg über die Vokabelarbeit anhand der Illustration von zwei aufeinanderzurasenden Herzen aktiviert den vorhandenen Wortschatz zum Thema *love, friendship* und *relationship*. Dieses Vokabular wird entweder an der Tafel oder auf einer Overhead-Projektor-Folie gesammelt. Der sich an diese Arbeit anschließende Dialog soll in Partnerarbeit verfasst und dann dem gesamten Kurs präsentiert werden.

Central Park at dusk
Sara Teasdale

Author
Sarah Teasdale (1884–1937) American lyrical poet. Throughout her life Sara suffered from poor health. She couldn't begin school until she was nine years old. In 1903 she graduated from Homer Hall. She was influenced by the British poet Christina Rossetti and numerous trips to Europe, beginning in 1905. In 1914 she married Ernst Filsinger who she divorced in 1929. In 1933 she committed suicide. Her last collection of poems, Strange Victory, was published posthumously in that year.

The poem
The title shows that this is a typical poem about nature, however, nature itself in Central Park (probably in Manhattan, New York) is mentioned only twice (leafless trees (l. 1), no sign of leaf or bud (l. 5)). The trees are illuminated by the light coming from the windows of the neighbouring houses and the streetlamps in Central Park. Combined with natural twilight an eerie atmosphere is created.
The structure follows this image through its irregular rhyme which becomes a partial rhyme when after the caesura at the end of line 6 the reader is reminded that the world is eagerly waiting for spring which will let nature appear in another light again.
The poet does not speak of individual people but of the whole world patiently waiting for spring; thus the last two lines of the poem lead to a generalisation and a deeper meaning of the poem.

Central Park at dusk

Unterrichtsempfehlungen

In diesem ersten Gedicht des Einführungsteils werden die Schüler/innen mit den Besonderheiten poetischer Ausdrucksformen und einigen stilistischen Mitteln wie „rhyme" und „imagery" (metaphor und simile) bekannt gemacht, worauf auch der Aufgabenapparat angelegt ist. Die Vermittlung bzw. Erarbeitung wird im Unterricht in die inhaltliche Erschließung des Gedichts integriert, die der Präsentation unmittelbar folgt.
Die Behandlung des Gedichts sollte folgende Schritte umfassen:

1. Präsentation bzw. Rezeption des Gedichts und Artikulation von Eindrücken

Die beiden Strophen werden bei geschlossenen Büchern zweimal langsam vorgetragen bzw. vom Tonträger präsentiert. Zuvor müssen die beiden im Schülerbuch definierten Wörter „to thread" und „gleam" erklärt werden.

Die ersten, sicherlich noch zaghaft formulierten Eindrücke und Besprechungsvorschläge werden an der Tafel festgehalten und nach der anschließenden individuellen Textrezeption bei geöffneten Büchern ergänzt. Folgende Äußerungen sind zu erwarten:

Board

> where is the park?
> poem describes a night in the park
> language different from everyday English
> why not title: a winter evening in Central Park?
> rhyme
> line "silent as women wait for love" not clear
> poem has two sections, a longer and a very short one
> atmosphere gloomy and melancholy

2. Inhaltlich-formale Analyse

Die genannten Eindrücke und Besprechungspunkte werden aufgegriffen, sie leiten die Analyse des Gedichttextes, wobei sich die Schüler/innen an folgenden drei Fragen orientieren können:

- What does the poet describe?
  (a) sichtbare Elemente des Parks; b) Atmosphäre und c) Reaktion von Menschen (s. oben: „Poem")). Die Beiträge könnten von einem Schüler skizzenhaft visualisiert werden:

Board

- What poetic and stylistic means does the poet employ?
  (poetische Sprache (Nennung von Beispielen), stilistische Mittel wie „metaphors" und „similes" (Nennung von Beispielen) sowie der sich der inhaltlichen Aussage anpassende Reim)
- What is the deeper meaning of the poem? (cf. Solutions)

Die Ergebnisse der Besprechung können (je nach Verlauf des Klassengesprächs) tabellarisch etwa so festgehalten werden:

Board: Summary of analysis

	level of mere description		level of deeper meaning
stanza/line	content	form	content + form
1 (ll. 1–5) (l. 6)	nature in winter mode, twilight ↓	(ll. 1–4) irregular rhyme	Even when a sombre phase appears to be almost endless, it is possible to hope for an improvement
2 (ll. 7–8)	eerie atmosphere, world waiting patiently for spring	(ll. 5–8) partial rhyme according to content	

Assignments – Solutions

1. Rewrite Sara Teasdale's poem in everyday English. Start like this:
There are buildings above trees that have lost all their leaves, they are very high. Soon the lamps are turned on and there is twilight and artificial light. Because it is winter, the trees have lost their leaves and everything is quiet. Everybody is waiting for spring to come.

Die Antworten variieren bei dieser Aufgabe natürlich, allerdings haben die meisten Schülerinnen und Schüler keine Schwierigkeiten, diesen kurzen lyrischen Text umzuformulieren.

2. Compare the poem and your version. What strikes you?

Whereas the prose version is nothing but a short description of an impression in Central Park in the evening, the poem conveys an atmosphere of loneliness and approaching spring.

3. A special feature of most poems is rhyme in different forms. What function may rhyme have in this poem?

In this poem the rhyme is irregular. a, b, c, b (irregular rhyme, first stanza); bud, love (partial rhyme second stanza) which stresses the eerie atmosphere of the poem – but finally e,e (everything, spring; regular rhyme again) which means that the reader is reminded that the world is waiting for spring. (cf. Unterrichtsempfehlungen)
In the first stanza there is no rhyme in *trees – out*, in the second stanza there is a partial rhyme in *bud – love*.

4. Find metaphors and similes in Central Park at Dusk.

> metaphors: l. 6 hush = silent, eerie atmosphere
> l. 7 silent = patient
> similes: l. 2 high as castles
> l. 7 silent as women
>
> These metaphors and similes are used to stress the poem's melancholy and eerie atmosphere.

The Passionate Shepherd to his love
Christopher Marlowe

Author
Christopher Marlowe (1564–1593) was born in Canterbury. Although his father was a mere shoemaker he attended King's School and was awarded a scholarship to Corpus Christi College in Cambridge. He was probably recruited for espionage work by the government. In 1587 he left for London where he became a playwright. In his six years as playwright he wrote important plays such as *The Jew of Malta* and *The Tragical History of Doctor Faustus*. He died after a quarrel over the payment of a pub bill.

The poem
The speaker of the poem, a young man, tries to persuade a young girl to fall in love with him and follow him to the countryside. There he wants them to share the pleasures of life in the country and to live in a simple style. The pleasures he describes include a beautiful landscape with valleys, hills and mountains, and rivers. He praises the birds' songs and promises to make her a bed of roses. For clothes he offers her fine wool garments decorated with flowers. He even promises shoes with gold buckles and buttons and clasps of coral and amber. Entertainment is guaranteed by the shepherds who are singing and dancing for them.

Unterrichtsempfehlungen

Als Einstieg könnte man die Schüler/innen bitten zu beschreiben, wie sie sich idealisiertes Landleben vorstellen, und einige Begriffe an der Tafel festhalten. Die Präsentation des Gedichts erfolgt bei geöffneten Büchern. Es wird Strophe für Strophe sukzessiv mit Pausen vorgetragen, in denen unbekanntes Vokabular erklärt wird, also im Sinn einer verzögerten Textrezeption, an deren Abschluss das Gedicht nochmals vom Tonträger zusammenhängend präsentiert wird.

Es ist zu erwarten, dass sich die Schüler/innen anschließend dahingehend äußern, dass es sich bei dem Gedicht inhaltlich um die Werbung eines jungen Mannes um die Gunst seiner Geliebten handelt, dass sich die Werbung aber recht merkwürdig vollzieht. Es ist leicht zu erkennen, dass

All you need is love – Poetry

die landbezogenen Bilder im Gedicht in einen Rahmen („Come live with me and be my love", erste Zeile) und („Then live with me and be my love", letzte Zeile) gesetzt sind, es sich also um einen „framed text" handelt.

Es empfiehlt sich, die einzelnen Bilder in einer Stillarbeitsphase Strophe für Strophe partnerweise erarbeiten, im Plenum beschreiben und mit einer in das Ergebnisraster einzutragenden Überschrift versehen zu lassen (s. unten).

Während bei dem Gedicht „Central Park at dusk" stilistische Elemente wie „metaphor" und „simile" in den Blick genommen wurden, liegt bei diesem Gedicht formal-methodisch der Akzent auf dem Versmaß, zu dessen Analyse auch Schülerlesungen gehören.

Die Ergebnissicherung der inhaltlich-formalen Analyse kann etwa so vorgenommen werden:

Board: Content and form of the poem

What the shepherd promises the girl (content)	How he tries to win her affection (form)
Come live with me and be my love 1. stanza — pleasures of country life 2. stanza — watching shepherds/listening to birds 3. stanza — beds of roses 4. stanza — beautiful clothes 5. stanza — beautiful clothes 6. stanza — entertainment by shepherds Then live with me and be my love	Reim + Versmaß eintragen

Die Fragen des Aufgabenapparats sind eine gute Nachbereitung des Unterrichtsgesprächs.

Assignments – Solutions

1. What does this poem describe?

> A young man wants to persuade a girl to become his lover. He tells her about all the pleasurable things that can be found in the country. He talks about the valleys and the fields and promises her that they will be sitting on the rocks and watching all the shepherds and sheep and listening to the birds. He promises her beds of roses and dresses.

2. In classical love poetry the poet often offers a woman the delights of the simple life. What are the pleasures Marlowe offers his lady?

> He offers her views of valleys, fields and rocky mountains (ll. 3/4), the songs of birds (l. 8) and a bed of roses (l. 9). He promises her clothes made of fine wool and decorated with flowers (ll. 11–14). Everything that he wants to give her is taken from nature like the belt of straw or the coral clasps (ll. 17/18). For entertainment he suggests young shepherds who will sing and dance for her (l. 21).

3. How does the poet combine the rural pleasures with the more sophisticated aspects? What does this tell you about the lady?

> Although the topic of the poem is rural life, there is nothing genuinely rustic in it. The poem is carefully constructed. It consists of six stanzas of four lines each with a mostly regular rhyme pattern of a, a, b, b. (Exceptions: eye rhymes: lines 1/2: love – prove, lines 7/8: falls – madrigals, 19/20 and 23/24: move – love; partial rhyme: lines 9/10: roses – posies.)
>
> The poem is in the pastoral tradition. Its vocabulary is not taken from real rural life but taken from the language of socially more sophisticated or even court life: madrigal (l. 8) fragrant (l. 10), embroidered (l. 12), buckles of gold (l. 16), coral clasps and amber bud (l. 18). There are a number of stylistic devices used that stress the poet's effort to woo not a naïve country girl but a more experienced lady.
>
> | | |
> |---|---|
> | l. 8 melodious birds sing madrigals | melodious refers to madrigals, not birds |
> | l. 23 mind may move | alliteration |
>
> The first line is repeated almost identically in the last line, the second line echoes and rhymes with the last but one line. The fifth stanza also ends with the first line preceded by the line *And if these pleasures may thee move* which resembles the third line of the sixth stanza *If these delights thy mind may move*, so there is a rise in meaning, the speaker moves from pleasures that are offered to delights.

4. Copy the first stanza and mark its lines to show the metre.

> There is an almost regular pattern of iambic tetrameters in this poem.
> In the third stanza there is an irregularity in line 10:
> *With a thousand fragrant posies*
> Here the first foot is a trochee.

5. How far do rhyme and rhythm support the poem's aim for simplicity?

> Although as we have seen the speaker is not addressing a simple girl, he pretends to be a country boy using a fairly regular pattern of rhyme and rhythm without many irregularities. So taken at face value the poem is written by a passionate shepherd who tries to persuade a country girl to be his lover.

6. Today young men do not chat up their girlfriends by evoking pictures from rural life. Write a text that would do the job of chatting up a girl nowadays.

> Answers could include invitations to cinema/ice-cream parlour/disco or offers to help with homework/computer problems.

Comeclose and Sleepnow
Roger McGough

Author
Roger McGough (born 1937) is one of the so-called Liverpudlian Mersey Poets. During the 1960s he worked as a teacher. He became a colourful member of the Liverpool pop culture, joining the pop group "Scaffold" and writing many of the lyrics for their songs. His collections include *Gig* (1973) and *Waving at Trains* (1982). He has also written several plays and some children's books. In 1997 he was made an OBE (Order of the British Empire) and in 2004 he was made a CBE.

The poem
The poem is written in free verse and achieves its effects only by grouping words and expressions together without any rhyme or metrical pattern. The scene described is loaded with guilt. A young man and a young woman have spent the night together, which will cause the girl to suffer from guilty pangs. The speaker of the poem is the young man who describes the feelings she will have in the morning after their lovemaking. He calls the sun a disguised policeman and the birds her disguised mother. He predicts that she will not spend any more time with him but will go home as fast as possible.

Unterrichtsempfehlungen

Durch die Kombination von Wörtern, die Neuschöpfung von Begriffen sowie stilistische Besonderheiten (grammatisch/syntaktive Unregelmäßigkeiten und „free verse" [muss zum geeigneten Zeitpunkt erklärt werden]) ist das Verständnis des Gedichts erschwert, und es bedarf daher anders als bei den beiden ersten Gedichten eines wohldurchdachten, schrittweisen Durchgangs durch den Text.

Es ist empfehlenswert, das Gedicht nach dem elementenhaft-synthetischen Verfahren zu besprechen, d.h. das Gedicht wird nicht als Ganzes präsentiert bzw. rezipiert, sondern einzelne Strophen bzw. Teile werden nacheinander nach dem Reihungsprinzip aneinandergefügt. Der Gedichttext wird zu diesem Zweck vom Lehrer auf Folie geschrieben; einzelne Teile werden nacheinander projiziert und besprochen.

Dabei ist zu beachten, dass das Verständnis wesentlich erleichtert wird, wenn das Gedicht in Sätze bzw. Teile aufgebrochen wird, was wegen des fehlenden Reims leicht möglich ist. In der nachstehenden Kopie des Gedichts sind mögliche Zäsuren angegeben.

Transparency:

	interpretation of the (different) parts ↓	grammatical structures and semantic deviations ↓
it is afterwards and you talk on tiptoe happy to be part of the darkness lips becoming a prelude to tiredness.		

Comeclose and Sleepnow for in the morning when a policeman disguised as the sun creeps into the room and your mother disguised as birds calls from the trees		
you will put on a dress of guilt and shoes with broken high ideals and refusing coffee run altheway home		

↑ Eintragung von Schülerbeiträgen ↑
(Möglichkeiten: s. h. Inhaltsangabe, Aufgabenlösungen und Lehrerinformationen)

Den Abschluss der Besprechung der einzelnen Teile, bei der Wörter bzw. Wortschöpfungen (z. B. broken high ideals, comeclose) und rhetorische Figuren (z. B. to talk on tiptoe, mother disguised as birds) erklärt werden müssen, bildet die zusammenhängende Präsentation des Gedichts über Tonträger.

Der Umfang der Bearbeitung der Aufgaben im Schülerbuch richtet sich nach dem Verlauf des Unterrichts.

Alternative: In leistungsstarken Kursen kann das Gedicht alternativ auch in Kleingruppen ganzheitlich-analytisch bearbeitet werden. Die Analyseergebnisse werden in ein Arbeitsblatt (Folienvorlage ohne die Zäsuren kennzeichnende Trennlinien) eingetragen, sodass – abhängig von den jeweiligen Ergebnissen – die zweite Lehrbuchaufgabe in der Nachbereitung evtl. entfallen kann.

Aufgabenstellung: Read the poem a few times and write down your general intuitive understanding of it. You will need this to refer back to as you go through the various stages of analysis. Divide the poem into different parts, analyse them and fill in your results in the worksheet. You may find that you need to change your first impression and interpretation, at least to some degree, in the light of the analysis.

Detailed information for the teacher

Grammatical structures

The second sentence of the poem contains a series of quite extensive grammatical parallelisms which it is important to understand. But it also turns out that the parallel items are semantically deviant, too. The parallelisms are (a) the two coordinated adverbial clauses in lines 9–14 and (b) the two coordinated noun phrases which are objects of the verb 'put' in lines 15–16.

Lines 9–14: when a policeman disguised as the sun creeps into the room and your mother disguised as birds calls from the trees
The predicate in the first of these clauses is the intransitive verb 'creeps' and the subject 'a policeman disguised as the sun', a noun phrase which has 'policeman' as its headword and contains a relative clause 'disguised as the sun' which postmodifies it. The adverbial prepositional phrase

'into the room' indicates the direction of movement. The second clause 'your mother disguised as birds calls from the trees' has the same structure, with the conjunction 'when' in line 9 clearly applying to this clause, too. The only difference is the adverbial, which indicates the source of the calling rather than its intended destination. This extensive parallelism suggests that we must see the policeman figure and the mother figure as equivalent to one another in some way. One obvious way to manage this interpretatively is to notice that they can both be figures of authority. The word 'mother' prototypically has kinder associations, but the parallelism and the fact that the clause about the policeman comes first tends to overlay the more positive connotations.

Lines 15–16: you will put on a dress of guilt and shoes with broken high ideals
The two noun phrases 'a dress of guilt' and 'shoes with broken high ideals' are both parallel in that they are both objects to 'put on'. In addition to that, both nouns ('dress' and 'shoes') are postmodified by a prepositional phrase.

Semantic deviations

Line 2: 'talk on tiptoe''
To walk on tiptoe is normal, but you clearly can't talk on tiptoe: This leads us to infer a metaphorical meaning that relates the semantically deviant line with the normal expression it is connected to (by the rhyme between 'talk' and 'walk' and the prepositional phrase, 'on tiptoe', which is common to both expressions). We walk on tiptoe when we are trying to be very quiet, so as not to disturb someone. Analogically, 'talk on tiptoe' suggests that the woman is whispering, or talking quietly, which increases the intimacy of the scene.

Lines 3–4: 'part of the darkness'
You can't literally be part of the darkness as human beings are physical objects and darkness is the absence of light. This phrase, like 'talk on tiptoe' which it is grammatically connected to, increases the feeling of intimacy which the young woman appears to feel.

Lines 9–14: when a policeman disguised as the sun creeps into the room and your mother disguised as birds calls from the trees
These are lines which we have already noticed as indicating, via parallelism, an 'authority figure' status for the mother as well as the policeman. If we take the first clause, the one involving the policeman, we can observe two important semantic deviations. First of all, the policeman is disguised as the sun. But it is very difficult to see how a policeman could possibly disguise himself as a star ninety-three million miles away from the earth. Secondly, in situational terms, it is difficult to believe that a policeman will creep into the room the next day. After all, as far as we know, the two lovers have not committed a crime. Indeed, it is much more plausible schematically, given the time of day, that the sun will creep into the room.

Once we have noticed this about the clause with the 'policeman' phrase as its subject, we can see that there are parallel oddities in the coordinated clause with the 'mother's phrase as its subject. The postmodifying relative clause has the same predicate, and the content of the 'as' phrase is also deviant in relation to the headword. It is almost as difficult to see how a mother could disguise herself as a flock of birds as it is to imagine how a policeman could disguise himself as the sun. And again, the headword-modifier relation seems to be the wrong way round. It is situationally unlikely that the young woman's mother will be calling from the trees, but birds typically do engage in such behaviour at dawn.

Clearly then, we need an interpretation that satisfies both the paralellisms already noticed and the semantic deviations pointed out here. A good way of satisfying all these dictates will be to notice that, when the young woman wakes at dawn, the sun and birds will remind her of her 'misdeed' and invoke fear of how others, particularly those she sees as authority figures (the police, her parents) will now regard her.

Lines 15–16: you will put on a dress of guilt and shoes with broken high ideals
'Dress of guilt' and 'shoes with broken high ideals' are both deviant semantically, which is reminiscent of the 'talk on tiptoe' deviation in line 2.
'Shoes' phrase: Shoes can't have broken high ideals as they are inanimate and so can't indulge in abstract thought. But you can have shoes with broken high heels, and like the 'talk'/'walk' rhyme relation 'heels' and 'ideals' also rhyme, linking 'shoes with broken high ideals' to the clichéd phrase 'shoes with broken high heels'. This gives rise to the idea that the young woman may indeed have shoes with broken heels (and so have difficulty in running home, even though she is so determined), and also that the broken heels symbolise the broken ideals.
'Dress of guilt': The parallel deviations give rise to the idea that the young woman's feelings of guilt, already awakened by the dawn, are increased as she gets dressed, thus motivating the helter-skelter run home described in the last lines of the poem. These aspects of the meaning of the text are not stated in the poem. Instead, we can infer the meaning via the parallelisms and deviations.

Assignments – Solutions

1. What strikes you when you read the poem?

> There is neither rhyme nor rhythm as in the poem by Christopher Marlowe. The author uses new combinations of words and even creates new words [to talk on tiptoe (l. 2), Comeclose, Sleepnow (l. 7), broken high ideals (l. 16), alltheway (l. 19)]. There are also typical poetic devices as repetition "disguised as" (ll. 10/13), metaphors "talk on tiptoe" (l. 2), "dress of guilt" (l. 15), "shoes with broken high ideals" (l. 16) and similes "disguised as the sun" (l. 10), "disguised as birds" (l. 13). This poem shows that poetic effects can be achieved without the traditional means of rhythm and rhyme.

2. Describe the love scene in your own words.

> A man is speaking to his girl-friend who does not live with him. They have just made love and he speaks to her shortly before she falls asleep. He knows that in the morning she will suffer from a bad conscience and will run home because the sun and birds will remind her of her mother who will not approve of her behaviour.

3. The poem contains a couple of metaphors and similes; find them. What function do you think these poetic devices have in this poem?

metaphors:
l. 2	talk on tiptoe
l. 15	dress of guilt
l. 16	broken high ideals

similes:
ll. 9/10	a policeman disguised as the sun
ll. 12/13	your mother disguised as birds

The metaphor *talk on tiptoe* stresses the girl's bad conscience – she does not talk loudly and self-confidently, but obviously she is shy and quiet. You can see her bad feeling about having made love to the speaker of the poem in the metaphor *dress of guilt*. Her *broken high ideals* – a pun on the expression high heels – show that she may have had different ideas about their relationship but was seduced by him.
The normal things that you can expect in the morning, namely the sun and the birds will have a different meaning for her – she will feel reminded of her guilt by them.

4. What may be the deeper meaning of the poem?

The poet wants to show the reader that illicit love will usually result in a bad conscience. However, it also becomes clear that the speaker of the poem does not think that he and his lover actually did anything wrong. So there is also the aspect of *carpe diem*.

Serious Luv
Benjamin Zephaniah

Author
Benjamin Zephaniah (born 1958) grew up in Jamaica and Birmingham. He left school at the age of 14 and moved to London where he published his first collection of poems in 1980. He works not only as a poet but also as a musician (*Us and Dem* 1990, *Belly of de Beast* 1996), playwright, actor and writer of children books (*Talking Turkeys* 1994 and *Funky Chickens* 1996). His most recent books are *We Are Britain* (2002) and *Chambers Primary Rhyming Dictionary* (2004).

The poem
The poem describes a young boy's first experience with love. The speaker of the poem is a schoolboy who has fallen in love with a classmate. He dreams about marrying her when they leave school. She is the only one who may call him Ben and he admires her schoolwork. She chews her pen in an attractive way and is very artistic in Art. She is beautiful in Biology and in Geography, she excels herself by helping him draw a map. He wants to use the time after school when they are walking home alone to propose to her. Unfortunately she tells him that she thinks he should take love more seriously and he now thinks he loves her friend.

Unterrichtsempfehlungen

Da die Gedichte „Serious Luv" und „First love" (vgl. auch S. 71) demselben Thema gewidmet sind, brauchen sie nicht unbedingt beide nacheinander im Plenum behandelt zu werden, sondern können in schüleraktivierender Weise arbeitsteilig bearbeitet werden.

Empfohlenes Verfahren:
1. Beide Gedichte werden in einer Still-Lesephase individuell zur Kenntnis genommen, unbekanntes Vokabular wird erklärt, sodass die Schüler/innen einen groben Eindruck von beiden Gedichten erhalten und sich anschließend für ein Gedicht entscheiden können. Es muss sichergestellt sein, dass die Aufteilung zu gleichen Teilen erfolgt.
2. In einer sich anschließenden Stillarbeitsphase beginnt jeder Schüler den Aufgabenapparat des von ihm gewählten Gedichts zu bearbeiten und beendet die Analyse in der Hausaufgabe.
3. In der Folgestunde werden die individuell ermittelten Ergebnisse verglichen, vereinheitlicht und die Präsentation im Plenum vorbereitet.
4. Diese sollte inhaltliche Aspekte und stilistisch-strukturelle Gesichtspunkte berücksichtigen, sodass nachfolgend Vergleiche möglich sind.
5. Beim Vergleich der beiden Gedichte werden in eine projizierte oder an die Tafel geschriebene Tabelle die herausgefundenen Gemeinsamkeiten und Unterschiede eingetragen.
6. Die in die Tabelle eingetragenen Resultate werden von den Schülern abgeschrieben; sie dienen als Hilfe für die sich anschließende Hausaufgabe, in der schriftlich beide Gedichte miteinander verglichen und kontrastiert werden. Eine Hilfe ist das nachfolgend abgedruckte Vokabelraster.

Tabelle: Serious Luv/First Love

	similarities	differences	
		Serious Luv	First love
content			
message/ deeper meaning			
structure			
stylistic devices			

Vokabelraster: Comparing poems
Both poems   are about …
                 refer to …
There are similarities between the poems along the following lines …

The first/second poem tells us about/deals with/describes … (begins/ends with …)
Unlike Zephaniah, Clare uses … in order to …/wants the reader to …
Clare describes/deals with/uses …, whereas Zephaniah speaks about/refers to …
In contrast to (author's name), (author's name) …

Assignments – Solutions

1. Who is the speaker in this poem?

> The speaker of the poem is clearly a very young boy who thinks he is in love for the first time. He does not really understand love as can be seen by the fact that he falls in love easily with another girl. He says "I think I luv" that shows the reader that he really is not very sure about his feelings.

2. Describe the speaker's feelings for the girl in his class.

> Answers will vary; however, it should be made clear that the little boy has a crush on his classmate.

3. Is his love returned?

> Obviously the girl says something to put the boy off since he decides to fall in love with her friend. Maybe the girl is a little more serious about the topic of love than the speaker of the poem.

4. The poem is called "Serious Luv". Comment on this title.

> You cannot take this title seriously because it is not about true love, but about a child's first love. The non-standard spelling 'luv' has a humorous effect on the reader. At the end of the poem the reader learns that the girl says the little boy should take love more seriously which offends him so that he leaves her and falls in love with her friend.

5. Where in the poem can you find repetition/anaphora?

> The phrase "I … luv de" can be found in lines 1, 6, 14 and 17.
> In lines 2 and 3 there is an anaphora: "I think"
> In lines 6, 7 and 9 the sentences start similarly: "When … do/does/doing."

6. Why does the author make use of this poetic device?

> This repetition shows that the speaker is a young boy who does not have an elaborate vocabulary. His experiences with the girl are restricted to school life, so he reports on her fabulous character traits in connection with her excellent school work. However, he seems to be really in love for the first time and not to be able to express himself in any other way.

7. What message do you think the author wants to convey to the reader?

> The author clearly wants to entertain and amuse grown-ups with this poem that maybe makes them remember their first crush on a schoolmate when they were young. On the other hand it shows how children take things easy and how easily their affections can be transferred. The non-standard spelling adds to the humorous effect.

First love
John Clare

Author
John Clare (1793–1864) was the son of an agricultural labourer and had virtually no schooling at all. His first publication in 1817 was self-funded, but was not a success. Because of his failure as a poet he had a mental breakdown in 1837 and was admitted to an asylum in Epping Forest. In 1841 he was certified insane and was committed to the Northampton Asylum. There he died in 1864.

The poem
The speaker of the poem is a young man who meets a young woman whose outward appearance causes him to fall in love with her at first sight. Unfortunately the young lady obviously does not return his feelings. Her only reaction to his admiring glances seems to be to wonder if something is wrong with him. His reaction towards this rejection is to blush and to feel as if everything around him becomes dark. But the young lady is still not moved to fall in love with him. He realises that he will never be able to fall in love like this again.

Assignments – Solutions

1. Describe in your own words the scene depicted by John Clare.

> The speaker of the poem meets a young lady with a sweet face. He at once falls head over heals in love with her. Unfortunately the young lady does not return his feelings. This is the reason why he blushes deeply and that he feels as if everything around him becomes like midnight. His blood burns around his heart which means that he suffers from physical discomfort. He feels rejected and realises that he will never be able to fall in love like that again.

2. Is his first love requited?

> The young lady sees him and feels that she has made a big impression on him, however, she misinterprets his stare and thinks something is wrong with her. It becomes clear that she does not respond to his feelings.

3. Explain the poet's use of metric pattern.

> The poet uses a fairly regular metric pattern of iambic tetrameters in the first stanza. Then the pattern becomes more irregular. In the second stanza there are alternating iambic tetrameters and trimeters with one irregularity in line 14 where the verse does not start with a iamb but a trochee (Words from). The third stanza consists of two iambic trimeters followed by one tetrameter and followed by another trimeter. In the fourth stanza there is a regular pattern of tetrameter – trimeter.

The reason for the irregularity in the metrical pattern is the turmoil in which the speaker of the poem finds himself after having fallen in love and being rejected at almost the same time.

4. Identify and explain the metaphors and similes the poet uses.

stylistic device	function
l. 1 struck (metaphor)	This metaphor describes how sudden and unexpected love hits the speaker like lightning.
l. 3 face bloomed like a sweet flower (simile)	This expression emphasises the young lady's beauty
l. 4 stole away my heart (metaphor)	This metaphor is almost a cliché because it has been used frequently to describe the feeling that one cannot help falling in love
l. 5 pale as deadly pale (simile) l. 8 life and all seemed turned to clay (simile).	Both expressions show how hopeless the situation is for the speaker. He uses the strong adverb "deadly" to stress his despair.
l. 14 words from my eyes did start (metaphor) l. 15 as chords from the string (simile)	This unusual combination of words and eyes puts stress on the fact that he is unable to speak because of the bolt that has struck him. The simile underlines this idea.
l. 16 blood burnt round my heart (metaphor)	Another strong metaphor which emphasises his pain: burning blood is a very strong way of saying that your heart aches because of unrequited love.
l. 17 flowers the winter's choice (metaphor) l. 18 love's bed always snow (metaphor)	These metaphors evoke a grim picture of pretty flowers being frozen in snow and winter weather. The flowers symbolise any hope of love and romance.
l. 23 my heart has left its dwelling-place (metaphor)	This metaphor shows that for the speaker this incident is not just a chance missed but signifies a change in his life. He thinks that he will never be able to truly fall in love again.

5. Compare the first four lines of the poem with the last four.

> In the first four lines of the poem the situation is described. The speaker has met a young woman for the first time and is totally erraptured. The adjective "sweet" is used twice, once in order to describe the feeling of love that strikes him and a second time to compare her face to a sweet flower (l. 3). The preposition "before" refers to his life before meeting her. The cliché "and stole my heart …" (l. 4) completes the description of this situation.
> In the last four lines of the poem the word "sweet" is again used to describe the girl's face (l. 21), but now the cliché is used to create a new original thought – the stolen heart is referred to one that has left its home and will never return. The "before" is also repeated – this time it is used as a preposition of place (I stood before).

6. Imagine you are the girl the poet has met. What does she write in her diary on that day?

> Answers will vary, however, students should realise that the encounter with the speaker of the poem has hardly made any impression on the girl. She just thought there was something wrong with him.

O when I was
A. E. Housman

Author
A. E. Housman (1859–1936) left Oxford without a degree because he had failed his final examinations. Having served 10 years in the civil service he became a professor of Latin at University College, London in 1892. In 1911 he became professor of Latin at Cambridge. He was one of the finest classical scholars of his time. During his lifetime only two small volumes of his poems appeared *A Shropshire Lad* (1896) and *Last Poems* (1922). His most characteristic themes are the passing of youth and the inevitability of death.

Unterrichtsempfehlungen

Die dem Gedicht beigegebenen Illustrationen Thurbers können in die Gedichtbehandlung einbezogen werden. Zunächst werden dann die beiden Cartoons unter Berücksichtigung folgender Aspekte im fragend-entwickelnden Verfahren analysiert:

- pictorial elements
- relationship between them
- graphic and pictorial presentation
- cartoonist's comment (message)

pictorial elements: ↑	pictorial elements: ↑
middle-aged man greeting lady politely; policeman, another lady, probably the first woman's mother, another man, dove, tree	policeman, two ladies and a man, same man in centre (sitting on bench, another woman on his lap), swinging a bottle of beer, probably drunk (hat crooked on head)
relationship between them:	**relationship between them:**
man in centre probably likes or loves lady; other persons amazed at his politeness; dove flying down: here symbol of peace and love; tree with leaves: sign of order	people standing around shocked, policeman seems to disapprove
graphic and pictorial presentation:	**pictorial presentation:**
funny drawing, man's politeness overdone (attracting viewer's attention)	exaggeration of man's unfeeling, inconstant behaviour, leaves falling from tree show that time has passed (spring-autumn)
cartoonist's comment:	**cartoonist's comment:**
Seems almost too good to be true!	How things can change!

Die anschließende Behandlung des Gedichts erfolgt anhand der Aufgabenstellung „Try to show that the two cartoons illustrate the poem appropiately". Die Schüler/innen setzen sich auf diese Weise in motivierender Weise mit dem Gedicht auseinander – eine lohnende Alternative zu bisherigen Verfahren der Gedichtinterpretation.

> Oh when I was in love with you,
> Then I was clean and brave,
> And miles around the wonder grew
> How well did I behave.
>
> And now the fancy passes by
> And nothing will remain,
> And miles around they'll say I
> Am quite myself again.

The first two lines show that love (when I was in love with you) can change somebody's behaviour (then I was clean and brave). The young man has changed completely like the man in the cartoon (other people were surprised to see him behave in a socially acceptable way). In the poem, this phenomenon is stressed by the structure 'when I …, then I …', in the cartoon by other people's reaction.

The cartoon as well as the poem show that a person's behaviour may change very soon when affection for another person fades: behaviour is as bad as before or even worse (poem: lines 5–8 describe that the young man has gone back to his former behaviour after his feelings for the girl have faded – cartoon: the cartoonist gets his message across by using symbols: tree leafless (symbol of time passing), dove (symbol of love and harmony) has disappeared, man drunk.

The two cartoons are an appropriate illustration for the poem.

Je nach Unterrichtsverlauf kann die erste Aufgabe des Schülerbuches entfallen.

Assignments – Solutions

1. What does the poet describe?

> A. E. Housman describes a man who obviously used to be some kind of rascal and who changed very much when he fell in love. Suddenly he could be very polite and take care of his outward appearance. However, when this temporary feeling passes he becomes his usual self again.

2. Why does a person change when falling in love?

> Here answers will vary, however, students should point out that different people might react differently to a new love. They could find answers such as:
> - realizing how good it feels to fall in love
> - meeting new people because of the new partner
> - trying to please a new partner by behaving better/taking more care over personal appearance/hygiene
> - …

3. Analyse the poem's language. What stylistic devices are used? Why?

> The author does not use many stylistic devices to describe the speaker of the poem as an easygoing young man whose behaviour is not always socially acceptable. The poem starts with an exclamation "Oh" (l. 1). There is an internal rhyme in the words "when" (l. 1) and "then" (l. 2) in order to stress the exceptional situation he was in when in love with the girl. The inversion in line 4 (did I behave) also stresses the unusual way he then behaved.
> In the second stanza when everything is back to normal he shows this by using the anaphora "and" in lines 5 to 7. The enjambment in lines 7/8 also underlines the fact that now he is – what else could the reader expect – his old self again.

Now that we've found love ...

Die Titelzeile des *Third World* Songs *Now that we've found love, what are we gonna do with it* soll die Schülerinnen und Schüler auf das Thema der folgenden Gedichte einstimmen, die sich mit dem Scheitern bzw. dem Erkalten von einst leidenschaftlichen Liebesbeziehungen beschäftigen. Diese Frage bewegt auch junge Leute, da in fast allen Familien Scheidungen und zerrüttete Beziehungen vorkommen.

Als Einstieg in die beiden Gedichte, die das Thema abgekühlte Liebe haben, dient der Vergleich der beiden Photographien des Paares, das deutlich den Unterschied zwischen Verliebtheit und abgekühlter Beziehung darstellt. In Partnerarbeit sollen Gesichtsausdruck und Körperhaltung der beiden verglichen werden.

Ending
Gavin Ewart

Author
Gavin Buchanan Ewart (1916–1995) was educated at Christ's College, Cambridge where he received a BA in 1937 and an MA in 1942. In 1939 his first volume *Poems and Songs* was published. After World War II he worked for several years as an advertising copywriter. In 1971 he became a full-time freelance writer.

Unterrichtsempfehlungen

Das Gedicht wird zunächst bei geschlossenen Büchern als „scrambled text" projiziert (Textstreifen auf Folie geschrieben oder auf die Projektionsfläche eines Overheadprojektors gelegt).
Folgende Vokabeln müssen erklärt werden: to congeal, chip, electric charge, inert, moored, to transmit, coy.

Transparency (scrambled poem):

The eyes that shone and seldom shut
are victims of a power cut.

The love we thought would never stop
now cools like a congealing chip.

The feet that ran to meet a date
are running slow and running late.

The kisses that were hot as curry
are bird-pecks taken in a hurry.

The hands that held electric charges
now lie inert as four moored barges.

The parts that then transmitted joy
are now reserved and cold and coy.

Romance, expected once to stay,
has left a note saying GONE AWAY.

Das Thema des Gedichts wird durch die beiden ersten und letzten Zeiten deutlich und durch seinen Kern (dazwischen liegende Textstreifen) exemplifiziert. Die Schüler/innen lesen die Textstreifen und äußern erste Eindrücke, z. B.:

- the poem deals with the ending of a love affair
- the poem describes how things have changed
- the poem uses humorous images, but may nevertheless be dealing with serious emotions

Die sich anschließende Aufgabe „How do you think the poet arranged the lines of the poem?" aktiviert die Schüler, die Puzzleteile des Gedichts zu ordnen und mit dem Original (Schülerbuch, S. 65) zu vergleichen. Es handelt sich hier um eine schüleraktivierende, andersartige Auseinandersetzung mit einem lyrischen Text. Die Schüler/innen lesen die Textstreifen mehrmals und lösen die Ordnungsaufgabe. Man wird feststellen, dass es eigentlich nicht nur ‚eine' unmittelbar richtige Lösung gibt, sondern vielmehr mehrere Möglichkeiten des Arrangements. Vergleiche unterschiedlicher Anordnungen bieten sich an.
Die Aufgaben 1 bis 4 im Schülerbuch schließen sich an.

Assignments – Solutions

1. Read the poem carefully. What aspects of a formerly "hot" relationship does the author talk about?

> In the poem the speaker talks about the following body parts and aspects of his relationship:
> hot kisses – bird-pecks (ll. 3/4)
> hands-electric charges – inert (ll. 5/6)
> feet running – slow (ll. 7/8)
> eyes bright – power cut (ll. 9/10)
> parts transmitted joy – cold and coy (ll. 11/12)
> What used to be full of romance and sexual tension is now no longer exciting or interesting – romance has left the relationship.

2. Find a suitable title for the poem.

> The students will find different titles for this poem. The poem's real title is "Ending". If none of the students has come up with a similar solution there can be a discussion about the "best" title.

3. How does the writer show that the relationship has suffered?

> As from line 3 on all the couplets rhyme you can see that the lack of rhyme in lines 1 and 2 (stop – chip) stress the contents of these lines, namely the fact that the formerly passionate love has cooled off considerably.
> Not only the rhyme pattern of the poem stresses the fact that the relationship has suffered, but also the use of comparisons between *now* and *then* presented in a regular pattern can emphasise the contrast between former passion and present indifference. Kisses hot as

curry (l. 3), hands that hold electric charges (l. 5), feet that run to meet a date (l. 7), eyes that shone and seldom shut (l. 9) and the parts that then transmitted joy (l. 11) speak of former sexual passion. This past passion is compared/contrasted with today's birdpecks (l. 4), moored barges (l. 6), slowly running feet (l. 8) and the eyes that are victims of a power cut (l. 10) because the spark has gone. There are strong similes and metaphors to describe the hopelessness of the situation.

4. Think of people whose love has suddenly or gradually come to an end.

Here answers will vary from personal acquaintances to the world of celebrities.

40 – Love
Roger McGough

Author
see "Comeclose and Sleepnow", p. 64

Unterrichtsempfehlungen

Vor der Behandlung des Gedichts sollte als *pre-reading information* die Zählweise beim Tennisspiel erklärt werden, z. B.:

15 – 0 = fifteen – love
15 – 15 = fifteen – all
30 – 0 = thirty – love
40 – 0 = forty – love

Anschließend lesen die Schüler das Gedicht individuell mehrmals und nennen Eindrücke und Besprechungspunkte.

Board

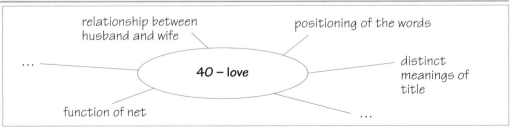

Die einzelnen, an die Tafel geschriebenen Punkte dienen als Basis für das Unterrichtsgespräch; die Aufgaben im Schülerbuch lehnen sich teilweise an das Unterrichtsgespräch an oder betreffen weitergehende Aspekte.

Assignments – Solutions

1. What do you learn about the state of this couple's marriage?

> Although the poem consists of only twenty words Roger McGough succeeds in conveying the impression that this couple has no romance or passion left because when they go home they are as separated from each other as when playing tennis.

2. How does Roger McGough convey the impression of a loveless marriage?

> McGough is able to create this impression by using the layout of the poem as a stylistic device. The way it is printed shows the fact that these two people are divided not only on the court by the real net, but also in all other situations of their lives by a symbolic net, namely their estrangement.

3. Is this text a poem?

> Students will discuss this topic and try to find out why a text like this can be truly called a poem.
> - close relationship between form and content
> - conveying a single thought by stylistic means
> - expressing complex ideas, namely the break-up of a relationship, with very few words
> - ...

You are the poet

An dieser Stelle können die Schülerinnen und Schüler selbst kreativ werden und sowohl *shape and concrete poems* als auch *acrostic poems* (die ersten Buchstaben aller Zeilen von oben nach unten gelesen ergeben einen Begriff) selbst schreiben und gestalten.

Unterrichtsempfehlungen

Zunächst sollten die Schülerinnen und Schüler die im Schülerbuch vorgegebene Skizze eines gebrochenen Herzens in ihre Hefte übertragen und dabei eventuell vergrößern. Es gibt nun zwei Möglichkeiten, diese Skizze mit Worten zu füllen – zum einen können die beiden Herzhälften mit Text gefüllt werden (*shape poem*), zum anderen können die Außenlinien beschriftet werden (*con-*

crete poem). Diese Aufgabe ist erfahrungsgemäß für die Schülerinnen und Schüler sehr motivierend, sie kann sehr gut in Partnerarbeit erledigt werden.

Acrostic poems sind Gedichte, deren jeweils erste Buchstaben jedes Verses von oben nach unten gelesen einen Begriff ergeben. Bei dem Beispiel im Schülerbuch ergibt sich das Wort *love*. Der Kurs kann nun aufgefordert werden, selbst ein Wort zu wählen und ein *acrostic poem* zu verfassen. Es sollte dabei beachtet werden, dass der Inhalt der Zeilen und der Begriff, der sich aus den ersten Buchstaben ergibt, inhaltlich miteinander verknüpft sind.

Besonders schön gestaltete Herzen oder gelungene *acrostic poems* können sowohl in der Klasse ausgehängt als auch in der Schülerzeitung veröffentlicht und somit angemessen gewürdigt werden.

Das Miniprojekt, einen selbstgewählten Songtext den Mitschülerinnen und Mitschülern zu präsentieren, soll auf das folgende Gedicht vorbereiten. Die Vorstellung von Popsongs wirkt auf Schülergruppen aller Leistungsniveaus erfahrungsgemäß sehr motivierend.

Als Hausaufgabe gibt man den Schülerinnen und Schülern die Aufgabe, in der nächsten Stunde einen Popsong vorzustellen, den sie besonders mögen. Sie sollen im Internet die *lyrics* des Liedes ausfindig machen und ausdrucken. Dann sollen sie einen kurzen Vortrag vorbereiten, in dem sie begründen, weshalb sie gerade dieses Lied ausgewählt haben. Dabei können sie sowohl auf die Musik als auch auf den Text eingehen. Das Lied soll auf CD mitgebracht und in der Stunde kurz angespielt werden. Man kann die Aufgabenstellung erweitern, indem man verlangt, dass kurze Informationen über die/den Interpreten bzw. Songschreiber gegeben werden. Ziel dieser Aufgabe ist, die Schülerinnen und Schüler dazu zu bringen, mehrere Minuten lang über ein sie interessierendes Thema reden zu lassen. Obwohl nicht alle Kursteilnehmer ihren Song vorstellen werden können, ist diese Aufgabe dennoch motivierend und man kann im weiteren Verlauf des Unterrichts immer wieder auf diese kleinen Kurzreferate zurückgreifen, sodass möglichst viele Schülerinnen und Schüler die Chance haben, über ihren Lieblingssong zu sprechen.

Additional poems

Poor girl
Maya Angelou

Author
Maya Angelou born 1928 in St. Louis, Missouri. Marguerite Johnson dropped out of high school and worked as the first black cable car conductor in San Francisco. She changed her name to Maya Angelou when she started performing at a nightclub in San Francisco. She enjoys a successful career as a singer writing her own lyrics and poems. In 1961 she moved to Africa where she lived for four years. Her first volume of poetry was published in 1971 (*Just Give Me a Cool Drink of Water 'Fore I Die*). At the inauguration of President Bill Clinton (1993) she recited her poem *On the Pulse of Morning*.

The poem

The speaker of this poem is a woman who has been left by her lover. He has found a new girl-friend and the speaker is quite sure that he will not stay with her either. She says that she would like to warn the new girl-friend, but that she realises that she would not be listened to. She addresses her former lover and tells him that she already feels sorry for his new girlfriend.

Assignments – Solutions

1. Why is the girl the poem is addressed to a poor girl?

> Contrary to the reader's expectation the narrator is not mad at her ex-boyfriend's new girl, but she feels sorry for her because she realises that he will leave her, too.

2. Who is the speaker of the poem?

> The speaker of the poem is a woman who realises that her partner has found a new love. She warns her successor of his unfaithfulness and that the man is a philanderer who is going to make her unhappy.

3. Maya Angelou's poetry is said to remind people of songs. Do you share this opinion? Listen to a reading of this poem and give reasons.

> - repetition of line two of each stanza
> - repetition of the last two lines of each stanza = chorus in a song
> - regular rhythm
> - easy words, a melody can be imagined
>
> Also the narrator herself says that the poor girl will "sing this song" (l. 28)

4. Explain the use of repetition in this poem.

> As mentioned before the repetition creates the impression that the poem could also be the lyric of a sad love song. In addition, the simple structure and the repetition help the reader to understand/to sympathise with the narrator's sad, cynical and resigned state of mind.

5. You are the *poor girl*. Answer the poet in a letter.

> Answers will vary.

Funeral Blues
W. H. Auden

Author
Auden, W(ystan) H(ugh) (1907–1973). Born in York, Auden achieved early fame in the 1930s as a hero of the left during the Great Depression. In 1939, he settled in the US and became a US citizen. Auden was not only a poet but also a playwright who collaborated with Christopher Isherwood. In 1936 he married Thomas Mann's daughter Erika. In 1948 Auden won the Pulitzer Prize.

The poem
In this poem the speaker mourns the death of his lover. It consists of a highly poetic list of items which the poet/speaker would like to be subdued or "turned off" so that they can share in his mourning.

Assignments – Solutions

1. What has happened to the speaker of this poem?

> The speaker of this poem is mourning his lover. He feels utterly devastated.

2. Who is invited to share the poem's mourning?

> The speaker yearns for absolute silence in his home; he does not want to hear the ticking of the clocks or the ringing of the telephone or the dog's barking and he most definitely does not want to hear any music.
> He wants planes to write the news in the sky and doves to wear black bows and policemen directing traffic to wear black gloves.
> He does not even want to see the stars or the moon or the sun. Oceans and forests are not wanted either.

3. What images does the poet create? Describe the effect on the reader.

> The poet uses a number of different images to emphasise his sense of loss.
> In the first stanza he is mainly concerned with sounds – he wants everything that can make a noise in his home to be silent. The telephone should be cut off (l. 1), and the piano should be silenced (l. 3). The second stanza deals with visual images. Planes should write *He is Dead* (l. 6) in the sky – the pronoun *He* implying that everybody will automatically know who is dead. The crêpe bows will naturally be black and form a contrast to the white necks of the doves. Traffic policemen usually wear white gloves when directing traffic, they should wear black gloves in order to demonstrate that they are also in mourning.
> In the last stanza the poet describes absolutely impossible tasks like putting out the stars

> (l. 14). The moon and sun are to be treated like boxes that can be packed away or machines that can be taken apart. He also wants to empty the ocean and sweep up the forest. Again theses images underline the speaker's terrible feeling of loss.

4. What could the initials W. H. of the author's name stand for?

> The initials W. H. stand for Wyston Hugh, a man's name. Surprisingly, the poem is not a woman mourning her husband or lover, but a man mourning his male lover's death.

Hier bietet sich folgende Hausaufgabe an, die den Kurs dazu zwingt, sich damit auseinanderzusetzen, dass man beim Thema Liebesgedicht fast zwangsläufig an Partnerschaften zwischen Männern und Frauen denkt:

In 2004 the BBC broadcast short shows called "Poetry". In each 15-minute show actresses and actors recited poems. One show dealt with the topic death. This poem by W. H. Auden was recited by an actress. Comment.

Der folgende Text stammt von Roger McGough und parodiert das Gedicht von Auden.

Stop All the Cars
(The Metro[1], 1980–1998, RIP[2])

Stop all the cars, cut off the ignition
Those who decide have made the decision
Muffle the exhaust, put flowers in the boot
Wear a black dress or morning suit.

5 Let the traffic lights remain on red
Jam the horns out of respect for the dead
Sound the Last Post and summon the guard
For the Metro has gone to the knacker's yard.

She was my rustbucket, my tin lizzie
10 She kept my garage mechanic busy
A tarnished icon of the Thatcher years
She ground to a halt as I ground the gears.

Traffic wardens openly break down and weep
Sleeping policemen stir in their sleep
15 Car thieves consider an easier trade
Ram-raiders can't be bothered to raid.

Close the motorways with black-ribboned cones
Riddle the ashes and rattle the bones
Sound the Last Post and summon the guard
20 For the Metro has gone to the knacker's yard.

---
[1] The Morris Metro was a not very successful car related to the Mini, but larger.
[2] Rest in peace

To my son
Thomas Hood

Author
Thomas Hood (1799–1845) was born as the son of a bookseller in London. He established himself as editor of a number of reputable periodicals and wrote much humorous and satirical verse.

The poem
In this poem a proud father praises his very young son as a very cute little fellow but on the other hand his loving and admiring thoughts are interrupted by his son's behaviour. The little boy is crying, trying to stick peas into his ears and even swallowing a pin. He is also about to fall down the stairs and to set his bib on fire. At the end of the first two stanzas he even spills the speaker's ink. At the end of the poem he is sent to his mother. The speaker wishes there were iron bars at the window and finally wants to send his son upstairs so that he can write his praises without further interruptions.

Assignments – Solutions

1. What affectionate terms does the author use when referring to or addressing his son?

> - happy, happy elf (l. 1)
> - tiny image of myself (l. 3)
> - merry laughing sprite (l. 5)
> - little tricky Puck (l. 9)
> - darling of thy sire (l. 13)
> - imp of mirth and joy (l. 15)
> - idol of thy parents (l. 17)
> - pretty opening rose (l. 20)
> - fresh as the morning and brilliant as its stars (l. 24)
> - bold as the hawk, yet gentle as the dove (l. 26)
>
> Generally speaking the author stresses how small (tiny, little imp) and how carefree and joyful (happy, merry, mirth and joy) his son is.

2. What situation is described in this poem?

> A family of three and a nanny called Janet are sitting at the table, probably having lunch or dinner. The poet is enjoying his son's presence and addressing him with a lot of loving names, however, the boy is very mischievous sticking peas into his ear, almost swallowing a pin, crawling near the stairs or playing with fire and spilling his father's ink and so on.

3. There are really two different texts interwoven in this poem. Explain this statement.

> Text one deals with the proud father addressing his son. The second text can be found in brackets (ll. 2, 4, 8, 12, 14, 17/18, 21, 23, 25, 27/28). It refers to the little boy's various pranks.

4. Guess the century this poem was written. Give reasons for your estimate.

> This poem was clearly written in the 19th century. You can see this not only because of the fact that a nanny is living with the family, but also because there are several expressions that are rather outdated:
> - thou (ll. 1, 3, 5, 9, 13, 15, 17)
> - sprite (l. 5)
> - with antic toys … bestuck (l. 10)
> - thy sire (l. 13)
> - pinafore (l. 14)
> - thy (l. 15/17)
> - imp (l. 15)
> - drat (l. 17)
> - morn (l. 24)

5. Analyse the poem's rhyme scheme and metric pattern (see Glossary p. 76). Explain its irregularities.

> The stanza's rhyme scheme is regular: a, b, a, b, c, c, d, d, e, e, f, f, g, g, h, i, h, i
> The metric pattern is also mostly regular, there are alternating iambic trimeters, tetrameters and pentameters, however irregularities can be found in lines 8, 14 and 18. In these lines the pattern is broken because there are exciting things happening that interrupt the speaker's train of thought. In line 8 he fears that his son will swallow a pin, in line 14 he thinks the little boy will set his pinafore on fire and in the last line the little boy has managed to knock over his inkpot.

6. These are three stanzas of a long ode. Write another stanza.

> Answers will vary.

For Heidi with blue hair
Fleur Adcock

Author
Fleur Adcock was born 1934 in New Zealand. Adcock spent most of her childhood living and studying in England. After World War II her family returned to New Zealand. She married the poet Alistair Campbell in 1952, had two sons and divorced him in 1958. In 1963 she returned with one of her sons to London where she worked as a librarian at the Foreign and Commonwealth Office. Since 1980, Adcock has worked as a freelance writer, producing her own poetry and translating and editing collections. She has published several collections of poems such as *The Eye of the Hurricane* (1964), *The Inner Harbour* (1979), *Looking back* (1997).

All you need is love – Poetry

The poem

In this poem the speaker is the father of a teenage girl who has just lost her mother. She is sent home from school because she has dyed her hair. She is very upset because her new hairdo was very expensive and she did not think that she was breaking any school rules. In the end the teachers give in. One of her black friends supports her by dying her hair as well.

Assignments – Solutions

1. Describe in your own words who the speaker's daughter is in conflict with.

> Heidi is in conflict with her teachers and the headmistress of her school. She is sent home and then talks to her father. She is very upset and cries because she feels unjustly treated.

2. What are the reasons for the conflict?

> Heidi has dyed her hair blue and paid a lot of money for her new hairdo. Unfortunately her teachers and her headmistress have sent her home from school because of her dyed hair, adding that her hair is not even in the school colours. It becomes apparent that Heidi is not only in conflict with her teachers because of her hair colour but also emotionally unstable because of her mother's recent death (ll. 20–22). It would be interesting to ask students why it would be "unfair" to mention the mother's death – the father wants to win the case on its merits without "special pleading".

3. Describe the poem's metric pattern and rhyme (see glossary p. 76).

> There is no rhyme or metric pattern to be identified in this poem. It is written in free verse.

4. Which features make this text a poem?

> The layout makes it clear that it is a poem although there is no rhyme and no metric pattern. Also typical stylistic devices such as repetition (ll. 10, 15, 26 school colours) or enjambment are used.

5. What does the poet think about teachers, school rules, etc.?

> He has a low opinion of them. They don't like students who step out of line/bend the rules, they 'twitter', but give in when faced by serious opposition.

6. Reading the poem out loud, how many voices could you use?

> You could use a speaker (father) and daughter, but you could also use more voices to include the headmistress. Students should be allowed to experiment.

7. Work in groups. Act out the scene in the kitchen. Use your own words.

> Students should present the results of their work in class.

For a good dog
Ogden Nash

Author
Ogden Nash (1902–1971). Born in Rye, New York, Ogden was a copywriter and then a member of the editorial staff of The New Yorker, before turning his talents full time to poetry. In 1925 he wrote his first children's book with Joseph Algers. In 1930 his first piece of satirical verse was published in *The New Yorker*. His turn of phrase, his puns, and his witty rhymes appealed to people of all ages.

The poem
In this poem the speaker compares his once wonderfully energetic dog with the way she is now. Ten years ago the dog was as fast as lightning and did not hesitate even to try and catch birds. The speaker says that ten years ago he himself also sometimes tried to do the impossible. Now, however, the little dog is half blind and bumps into things. She seems to be ready to die. The speaker realises when watching the dog that he must also die sooner or later.

Assignments – Solutions

1. Which characteristics of his dog does the author praise?

> The speaker of the poem remembers how lively and energetic his dog used to be. She could run very fast and had bright eyes. He admired her energy and speed.

2. What changes have taken place?

> Whereas the dog was very fast and energetic ten years ago, she is now very slow and knocks against a chair because she is half-blind. Instead of running as fast as lightning she now seems to realise herself that she is close to death.

3. Analyse the poem's rhyme scheme (see glossary p. 76).

> Rhyme scheme: 1. stanza: ababcbdb; 2. stanza: ebebfbfbgbgbhbhb
> The recurring rhyme "b" holds the structure of the poem together.
> The constant change of rhyme corresponds to the dog's changing behaviour in her life.

4. Which stylistic devices does Ogden Nash use to illustrate his love for his dog and his thoughts about approaching death?

> When the speaker describes his dog he uses metaphors to describe her energy and power. In lines 3 and 4 he says that her backbone was a bow and her eyes were arrows. He says that she split the air (l. 17) which illustrates the dog's speed. When reminiscing about the dog

ten years ago he repeatedly compares her with himself: ll. 7/8, ll. 15/16 where he says that not only his dog was younger and could do great things, but so could he.
Consequently, when he thinks about the approaching death of the dog he also thinks of his own death.

Thematic vocabulary: love – friendship

	term	expressions	
love	love	to be in love with sb.	**Topic:**
		to fall in love with sb.	**love – friendship**
		to love sb. dearly	
		to grow to love sb.	
		love at first sight	
		to be madly in love	
		the love of your life	
	devotion	to give sb. years of devotion	
		to be devoted to	
	affection	to show affection	
		affection for	
		to be affectionate towards	
friendship	friendship	to make friends with sb.	
		to strike up a friendship	
		to befriend	

I am very bothered
Simon Armitage

I am very bothered when I think
of the bad things I have done in my life.
Not least that time in the chemistry lab
when I held a pair of scissors by the blades
and played the handles
in the naked flame of the Bunsen burner;
then called your name, and handed them over.

O the unrivalled stench of branded skin
as you slipped your thumb and middle finger in,
then couldn't shake off the two burning rings. Marked
the doctor said, for eternity.

Don't believe me, please if I say
that was just my butterfingered way, at thirteen,
of asking you if you would marry me.

butterfingered
clumsy

Assignments
1. Retell in your own words the incident the poet describes in this poem.
2. Name and explain the stylistic devices the poet uses.
3. You have a choice here:
    a) Compare this poem to Benjamin Zephaniah's poem "Serious Luv".
    b) You are the girl whose hand has been burnt. Write a letter to the speaker of the poem in answer to his poem.

Solutions

1. The speaker of the poem looks back on his youth and realises that there are many things in his life he is ashamed of. The incident happened when he was thirteen years old. He had a Chemistry class with a girl he fancied. He took a pair of scissors by the blades and held the handles in the flame of a Bunsen burner and then he handed them to the girl. Of course, the girl's hand was badly burnt and she had to be taken to a doctor who said that she would have the scars for life.

2. Students should point out that this poem is written in free verse. The first stanza is almost a prose rendition of what happened years ago when the speaker and the woman were still children. The 'o' in l. 8 is the speaker's shocked reaction when he realises what he has done. However, the word 'unrivalled' suggests that, in a rather twisted way, he quite enjoyed the incident at the time.
   The enjambment in lines 10 and 11 emphasises how badly the girl was burnt and how she was "marked" by the speaker's prank.
   The unusual request not to believe him (ll. 12) shows that the speaker actually thinks that he wanted to tell his classmate that he loved her, but feels embarrassed by his younger self.

3. a) Students should point out that Zephania's poem is a text reporting the thoughts of a young boy who is very insecure about his own feelings and is not yet able to realise what love means. In Armitage's poem, however, an adult reflects on an incident from the past and tries to apologise for a case of bad behaviour when he was at school.
   b) In the letter the woman should point out how badly the burn had hurt. It depends on the student's point of view if she can forgive the speaker of the poem or not.

Where does Britain belong? – Non-fictional texts

Funktion und Aufbau des Kapitels

Im Englischunterricht werden neben literarischen Texten besonders in thematisch angelegten Unterrichtsreihen nicht-fiktionale Texte behandelt. Es ist daher das Ziel dieses Kapitels, Techniken vorzustellen und einzuüben, die für die Analyse und Kommentierung sog. Sachtexte geeignet sind. Nicht-fiktionale Texte lassen sich in eine Vielzahl von Texttypen und Textformen einteilen, von denen allerdings eine Reihe im Englischunterricht eine untergeordnete Rolle spielen wie z. B. Lexikoneinträge, Kochrezepte, Bedienungsanleitungen für elektrische Geräte usw. In dieses Kapitel sind daher nur solche nicht-fiktionalen Texttypen und deren untergeordnete Textformen aufgenommen worden, die in Unterrichtsmaterialien für den Englischunterricht in der Sekundarstufe II integriert sind und die zu lesen und zu analysieren vordringlich ist (vgl. glossary: Non-fictional text types, Students' Book, p. 106).

Die einzelnen Texttypen und Textformen werden nicht in einer bestimmten, linguistisch ausgerichteten Reihenfolge behandelt, sondern ordnen sich dem landeskundlichen Thema unter. Thematisch geht es um das Verhältnis Großbritanniens zu europäischen Staaten, im weitesten Sinn um den europäischen Gedanken schlechthin. Das Kapitel beginnt mit einem kurzen historischen Abriss des Verhältnisses zu den Vereinigten Staaten und einer knappen Überleitung zum Verhältnis zu Europa, das Gegenstand der folgenden Unterkapitel und Texte ist.

Im Diagramm lässt sich der Aufbau des Kapitels so darstellen:

Britain's position in the world

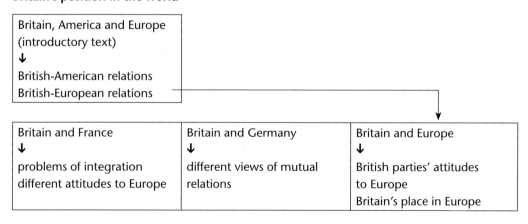

Introduction

Assignments – Solutions

Brief introduction to the unit with visual support in cartoon form. British people feel close to the US in some ways, but want to keep their distance in others. The situation in connection with the EU is similar. In the nineteenth century Britain was quite happy to remain in 'splendid isolation' as far as Europe was concerned.

Solutions

Map 1: Reasons for feeling close to the US:
Same language, shared history/literature, many shared ideals, popular holiday destination, family links past (as a result of emigration) and present (emigration, business)
Reasons for keeping distance: Danger of American popular culture/popular music/language features swamping British culture, dislike of some American stereotypes, disapproval of some aspects of American foreign policy.

Map 2: For and against the EU:
For: large market for British goods, need for European unity to compete with the US, China, India. National units too small in a global economy.
Against: Fear of the common currency (euro), fear that sovereignty will be lost, fear that France and Germany run the show, British economy has performed well in comparison with the Eurozone in recent years (lower unemployment rates, for example), belief that one interest rate for all cannot be a good thing.

Map 3: Splendid isolation:
Britain had much closer links with its empire than with Europe in those days. Was thankful to keep out of complicated European alliances and wars. The French seen as archetypal foreigners and traditional enemies. This kind of attitude would be impossible nowadays. The empire has gone, and thousands of British people live in France or travel there on a regular basis.

Britain, America and Europe

The British Dilemma

Anthony Sampson

The text
During the early postwar years British politicians saw ties with America and the Commonwealth as paramount, while links with Europe were also being forged, in spite of de Gaulle's opposition to British entry. Edward Heath eventually took Britain into Europe. Although he did not think that

links with America were of very much benefit to Britain, he and subsequent prime ministers right up to Tony Blair, still felt strongly that there was some kind of 'special relationship' with the Americans, and were unwilling to throw in their lot with Europe in a wholehearted kind of way. However, European influence was spreading into Britain irresistibly, like the tide coming in. Brussels bureaucrats were blamed for introducing European measures which were in fact fully supported by the British government.

Unterrichtsempfehlungen

Der Text schließt sich unmittelbar an die erste Rubrik der Einstiegsseite mit dem Hinweis auf die Bindungen zwischen Großbritannien und den Vereinigten Staaten an. Der Untertitel „The British Dilemma" weist auf Schwierigkeiten hin, in die sich Großbritannien hinsichtlich seiner Beziehungen zu den Vereinigten Staaten gestellt sieht.

Vor der Lektüre des Textes sollten die Schüler und Schülerinnen in einer Art pre-reading-Aufgabe den Untertitel „The British Dilemma" mit der Hauptüberschrift „Britain, America and Europe" in Beziehung setzen, überlegen, worin das Dilemma bestehen könnte, und Fragen formulieren, die sie durch den Text beantwortet haben möchten.

Da der Text durch eine Vielzahl von Namen und Fakten belastet ist, muss er langsam und gründlich gelesen werden (vgl. *intensive reading*, Students' Book, S. 135). Falls möglich, sollten wichtige Fakten unterstrichen bzw. in Randbemerkungen festgehalten werden, damit sie für die Besprechung im Plenum präsent sind. Die von den Schülern ohne Lehrersteuerung genannten Fakten werden an der Tafel stichwortartig festgehalten und anschließend in die Chronologie, d.h. die Struktur des Textes gebracht, was eine wesentliche Hilfe für die Erledigung des Aufgabenapparats bedeutet.

Board: Structure of the text

- Introduction:
  Over forty years, prime ministers have been drawn towards both America and Europe. (ll. 1–2)
- Macmillan:
  equal links to America and the Commonwealth (ll. 3–9)
- Macmillan's successors:
  pro USA (9–10)
- Edward Heath:
  in favour of Europe (ll. 10–13)
- Blair and predecessors:
  "special relationship" with America (ll. 13–24)
- since entry into European Community:
  stronger links with Europe (ll. 25–40)

Assignments – Solutions

1. What did Macmillan think about

  1. the Common Market/Europe?
  2. the Commonwealth?
  3. America?

> 1. Macmillan was in favour of the Common Market/Europe.
> 2. He also regarded the Commonwealth as important.
> 3. America was seen as of equal importance with the Commonwealth.

2. What did Heath think about the so-called 'special relationship' with America?

> Heath did not think that Britain got anything in return for her loyalty to the US. The so-called 'special relationship' was largely one-way, and not regarded as very important by the Americans.

3. How have most British Prime Ministers and other politicians felt about America in the past?

> They have still regarded America as a very important ally, and felt safe under the protection of the world's most powerful nation.

4. How has the situation changed in recent years?

> Links with Europe and European influence have slowly but surely become stronger, often without ordinary people realising what was happening.

5. What aspects of the text tell you that Sampson is or has in the past been close to the centres of power in Britain?

> He uses expressions such as "he (Macmillan) told me". He speaks throughout as if his information about politicians etc. is absolutely reliable, 'straight from the horse's mouth'.

Cartoon: 4 more years

Die Analyse des Cartoons, der die Besprechung der britisch-amerikanischen Beziehungen aus amerikanischer Sicht abschließt, wird Schülern mit geringer Erfahrung mit dieser visuellen Textform vermutlich, möglicherweise auch wegen fehlenden landeskundlichen und politischen Basiswissens, Schwierigkeiten bereiten.
Er sollte daher im fragend-entwickelnden Verfahren erschlossen werden, d. h. durch geeignete, den Analyseprozess steuernde Lehrerfragen. Diese müssten folgende drei Bereiche abdecken:

Content: What the cartoon is about
Analysis: Description of the cartoon (Elemente und deren Beziehung zueinander; Denotation symbolhafter Elemente), Botschaft des Cartoons
Evaluation: Opinions of the cartoon

Für die Analyse von Cartoons sollten die Schüler/innen eine Kopie des nachstehenden Analyserasters erhalten.

Board: Working with cartoons

Step 1: Content
- What is the cartoon about? (Look at caption or newspaper article which the drawing goes with.)

Step 2: Analysis
- What does the cartoon show in the foreground, background and centre? (pictorial elements, relationship between them, what they stand for)
- What does the cartoonist criticise or comment on? (cartoonist's message)

Step 3: Evaluation
- Do you think the cartoon achieves its aim?

Symbols used and their significance:
covered wagon – powerful symbol of the early American settlers who crossed the country to the west (Oregon trail) in these vehicles.
Poodle – used in a humiliating way to symbolise Britain's 'dog-like' devotion to America. The rope emphasises Britain's powerlessness in this relationship. The British poodle is suggesting some policies which Britain would like America to follow during Bush's second period of office, but it is quite clear that none of them will have much priority in the White House.

Additional questions and answers for the cartoon:
1. What exactly can you see in the cartoon?
    a *Planwagen* (covered wagon)
2. Who's driving it?
    President George W. Bush
3. What is the wagon pulling?
    a dog (poodle)
4. What do the covered wagon and the poodle represent?
    The covered wagon respresents the US, and the poodle represents Tony Blair, and also, to some extent, Britain.
5. What does the choice of these symbols tell us about the (cartoonist's view of the) relationship between the two countries?
    Britain powerless compared with the US/humiliating relationship/Bush does not listen to Blair/his British ally
6. How do you think Mr Blair might react to the cartoon?
    angry/humiliated/would regard it as very unfair/would say that it misrepresented the true relationship between the two countries/would try to give examples of British influence on American policies.

Switchboard for talking about the cartoon:
This cartoon by … shows … (straightforward description of the drawing)
It looks/doesn't look as if the cartoon is intended to be … funny/satirical/serious/political
I think the cartoonist is commenting on … a political issue/something in the news/a social issue/ the way celebrities behave/a sporting event
He gets his message across by using … symbols/caricatures/well-known objects/speech bubbles
These (symbols) represent …
The choice of these particular (symbols) shows that the cartoonist … likes/dislikes/disapproves strongly of/wants to ridicule/satirise …
The point of the cartoon is … to make people more aware of …/to attack arrogance/incompetence/pompousness …/to amuse/annoy/provoke people

Britain and France

Photo

Assignments – Solutions

1. Describe the photo, and try to explain exactly what photos like this could mean for English people.

> The photo shows (a British view of) the typical Frenchman, looking relaxed in his standard beret and holding a glass of red wine. This kind of photo symbolises a version of the 'good life' which is very appealing for British people. It includes better weather, better food, a better, more relaxed way of life, and above all, cheap wine.

2. Prosperous English people often move to France and start a new life there – like the author of the article which follows. What do you think attracts people like her?

> The attractions are those described above, plus the fact that very high British house prices have made it possible for many middle-class British people to buy a house in France on favourable terms. This gives them high status with the neighbours, an additional attraction.

Bonjour Mate
Helena Frith Powell

The text
The author begins with some advice to expatriate British people who have moved to France or are planning to do so. She thinks it is very bad that so many British people do not bother to learn French and tend to mix only with other Brits. She wonders how the French feel about these attitudes, and has tried to set a better example herself by listening to French radio stations and arranging for one-to-one French lessons. Her husband has helped her family to integrate by joining a cycling team. The Frith Powells invited the team to an English breakfast, and were in return invited to a retirement party for another member of the team, most of who are over 60 but very fit. This marvellous, typically French garden party lasted all day. The author feels that it would have been terrible to live next door and not to have been invited.

Unterrichtsempfehlungen

Das mit einem Fragenapparat versehene Photo eröffnet den Einstieg in den nachfolgenden Zeitungsartikel, der ein prägnantes Beispiel dafür ist, wie sich eine britische Familie im Ausland, hier Frankreich, integrieren kann. Er zeigt Wege für das Zusammenleben von Menschen unterschiedlicher Herkunft auf, ein brennendes Problem im heutigen Europa.
Für die Präsentation dieses in narrativer Form verfassten Zeitungsartikels bietet sich die (möglichst zweimalige) auditive Darbietung an. Obwohl der Text sprachlich recht einfach ist, sollte der auditiven Darbietung doch die Erklärung einiger unbekannter Wörter vorangehen. Das Hörverstehen selbst kann durch eine *notetaking*-Tabelle gesteuert werden, die die Schüler und Schülerinnen während des Hörens und nach dem Hören ausfüllen.

Note-taking table: Moving from Britain to France

basic requirements for integration	the author's integration strategy
....	↓
negative examples	learning the language
....	making friends
....	....
	....

Nach der auditiven Darbietung und der Analyse des Inhalts anhand der ausgefüllten *note-taking*-Tabelle wird der Text nochmals lesend zur Kenntnis genommen. Im Vordergrund steht nun die ausführliche Besprechung struktureller und sprachlicher Aspekte als Grundlage für das Verfassen eines eigenen Zeitungstextes. Die Ergebnisse können stichwortartig an der Tafel festgehalten werden (siehe Lösungsvorschlag, S. 98 f.).

Assignments – Solutions

1. In the author's view, what are right and wrong ways to go about living in another country? Make lists of "do's and don't's":

Do's	Don't's
learn French	remain monolingual
escape from British enclaves	use sign language in French shops
integrate/make friends with the neighbours	mix only with other Brits/go to all-British barbecues
avoid all-British barbecues	see no reason to integrate/try to do things the French way
join some kind of French club/activity group or sports team	

2. To what extent does the author accept the idealised view of France referred to at the beginning of this section?

She accepts it wholeheartedly, commenting favourably on French food and drink, way of life, living outside in the sun, love of cycling.

3. What features of a typical newspaper column can you find in the text above? The article contains the following elements typical of a column:

- very personal, subjective, lively style
- includes personal opinions vigorously expressed
- deals with the author's own/her husband's life/experiences
- it gives interesting detailed information about life in France, including French customs, typical food and drink, etc.

4. Write your own newspaper column based on some interesting observations you have made about the area and/or the people on a holiday in Germany or abroad.
Some hints:

- Ask yourself exactly what aspects of the situation you want to describe can be made interesting for the reader – jot down a few notes and put them in a logical order.
- Start with something exciting/provocative/unusual – you could ask readers a question as Helena Frith Powell does.
- Include plenty of detail, direct speech, etc.
- Don't be afraid to exaggerate a bit. Professional journalists do, too.
- Try to find a striking sentence for the conclusion.

France's vision is not ours
Anatole Kaletsky

Reading task – Solution
As you read the text. Try to find out why France is reasonably happy to be an integral part of Europe, while Britain is not.

> France is on the mainland, has lost its global role and sees a more promising future for itself in Europe as a counterbalance to America.
> Britain is an offshore island, has a strong sense of national identity, and sees itself to some extent as part of a global culture led by America, in spite of widespread disagreement on some issues such as the invasion of Iraq.

The text
Britain's main problem with Europe is that it refuses to identify itself as a European nation. Over the years, many other European nations, particularly those with a troubled past, have begun to feel a European sense of identity.
This has not happened to the same extent in nations with strong sense of national identity, such as Britain. The French also have this strong sense of national identity, but nevertheless feel European. Earlier this could have been put down to the fact that the French thought they could run Europe with Germany paying the bills, but nowadays French officials do not dominate the EU any more. One might think this will make the French feel more Eurosceptic, but this is unlikely for three reasons, all of which demonstrate how different French and British attitudes still remain.
The first reason is that **1) Britain has always been peripheral to Europe and thought in more global terms than France. 2) Britain is also fortunate to speak the global language and share in the dominant culture, whereas the French language and French culture have become less universal.** The final reason is that Britain is out of line in its attitude to America, too. The rise of other forms of civilisation to challenge that of Europe is important in the longer term, but at present Britain's main problem is that the rest of Europe is beginning to see America as an alien civilisation in some ways. **3) The French President believes that Europe needs to act as a counterweight to America. Britain's Prime Minister, if not all his subjects, is firmly on America's side.**

Cartoon
Students could be asked about their views on doubtful refereeing decisions, giving examples, and also discuss whether television footage of doubtful events on the field should be consulted by referees before they make their decisions.

Unterrichtsempfehlungen

Dieser recht schwierige Text über Großbritanniens und Frankreichs Verhältnis zu Europa bedarf eines gründlichen Textstudiums. Empfehlenswert ist die Behandlung in zwei Schritten: 1) ll. 1–32,

2) ll. 33–78. Der Leseauftrag in der Randspalte leitet die Schüler an, auf wesentliche Fakten zu achten.

Der erste Teil kann als Hinführung zur Begründung der Titelaussage betrachtet werden. Nach einleitenden Bemerkungen zur Notwendigkeit eines *shared sense of identity* wird Frankreichs Position zur EU untersucht.

Die Schüler und Schülerinnen sollten, da das Buch nicht in allen Fällen ihr Eigentum sein wird und damit Unterstreichungen und Randbemerkungen zu unterlassen sind, ein Formblatt an die Hand bekommen, in das sie die wesentlichen Fakten eintragen.

Part 1 (l. 1–l. 32)		
European unification	sense of national identity	
sense of European identity		
....		
....	....	....
Part 2 (ll. 33–78)		
Differences between French and British attitudes to Europe		
....	....	....
....	....	....
etc.	etc.	etc.

Die Untersuchung des Textes auf *facts* und *opinions* (Eintrag in zwei Kolumnen) mit Rückgriff auf die Info-Box sowie auf sprachliche Besonderheiten schließt sich an die Inhaltsanalyse an.

Assignments – Solutions

1. Explain in a short paragraph, what the text is about, emphasising the contrasts which Kaletsky sees between the French and English positions on Europe.

> See the summary above. Contrasts are printed in bold italics.

2. Go through the text, and try to find as many examples as you can of **facts** and **opinions**. Set out the results in two columns, using the first few words of each item to identify it.

> This is a difficult task for students because although most people would agree with much of what Kaletsky says, there are not many hard facts for the left-hand column.

Facts	Opinions
Europe's economic performance has waned.	Britain does not have a strong European identity.
France, like Britain has a long history, a strong national culture and strong central government.	Some countries are more Eurosceptic than others.

France loses a lot of battles in Brussels nowadays.	The French are unlikely to turn Euro-sceptic.
Britain's interests have been mainly global for a long time.	The gulf between French and British attitudes will widen in the future.
Britain is at the periphery of Europe.	Britain was never going to immerse itself in Europe with the same enthusiasm as France.
Britain speaks the world's main international language.	
French has become less important as an international language.	
...	...

3. Outline the three reasons which Kaletsky gives to support his view "that the gulf between French and British attitudes to Europe will widen rather than narrow in the years ahead."

The three reasons are numbered in the summary above.

4. This is definitely not a sensational article, but Kaletsky nevertheless uses some **emotional language** to reinforce his arguments. Try to find some examples.

Examples of emotional language:
a) fatal flaw (l. 7)
b) hard to sell (l. 13)
c) a glorious national culture (l. 19)
d) the gulf between French and British attitudes (l. 37)
e) the slogan ... became an obsession (l. 41 f.)
f) was eclipsed by Britain (l. 53)
g) a bastion against the hegemony of Anglo-Saxon culture (l. 56 f.)
h) the widening rift (l. 59)
i) not necessarily doomed to failure (l. 61)
j) no more noticeable than the air we breathe (l. 63 f.)
k) an alien, even hostile civilisation (l. 69)
l) building a bridge to nowhere (l. 73 f.)

5. What do you think the final phrase in the article, "a bridge to nowhere" refers to here?

It seems as if Tony Blair wants/wanted the best of both worlds. He wanted to build a better bridge to Europe (but always held back when it really mattered, as in the case of the Euro), and he was firmly on America's side, too, but did not really have the country behind him. So neither of his two 'bridges' reaches across to firm ground on the other side.

6. Write a short comment about German attitudes to Europe in a similar style to that used by the author. It would be a good idea to collect useful expressions for this kind of text.

> Personal comment. Some ideas:
> - Germany accepts that it is a fully European country, and is in fact the largest European economy and has the largest population (until or unless Turkey joins the EU).
> - National sense of identity damaged by the war etc., so it was perhaps easier to think in European than in nationalist terms in the past. This may be changing. Danger that patriotism may be taken over by right-wing parties.
> - doubts over further expansion, particularly the inclusion of Muslim countries
> - not much help from the rest of Europe with solving East-West problems
> - The euro is blamed for rising prices, but is accepted as a replacement for the D-mark without much enthusiasm.
> - There is a suspicion that Germany has to pay more than its share of the EU's bills.

Britain and Germany

Two kinds of spitfire

Advertisement
How do Brits feel about Germany (and vice versa), more than sixty years after the the end of the Second World War?

Possible responses:

> Brits – Germany
> - still seen by some people, not all of them old, as the former nazi enemy
> - lack of first-hand knowledge about Germany
> - not very many British visitors to Germany
> - German cars enjoy high status (and can give rise to envy among those who can't afford one)
> - history teaching concentrates too much on the war
> - not many students learn German
> - World football championship in 2006 had a positive effect on Germany's image in Britain
>
> Germans – Britain
> - seen as something of an outsider in the EU (insularity)
> - views dominated by school textbooks
> - London/some holiday destinations covered in school
> - Britain apparently doing well economically
> - but believed as well to have all kinds of social problems
> - The English language is taught in all secondary schools

Assignments – Solutions

1. What is the English name for this game? And the American name?

> BE noughts and crosses, AE Tick-tack-toe

2. Explain how the game is played.

> Two pairs of parallel lines are drawn at ninety degrees across one another.
> One player draws noughts, and the other draws crosses in the resulting nine squares. The first player to complete a straight line of three noughts or crosses in any direction wins.

3. What symbols are used here? What do they represent?

> The symbols used here are the forms of the national flags of Britain ('noughts') and wartime Germany ('crosses') as displayed on the wings of warplanes. The symbols represent the planes of the two countries (typically Spitfires and Messerschmidts) during the Second World War.

4. Explain the significance of the diagonal line, both in the game, and in a figurative sense.

> In the game the winner sometimes draws this kind of line to show that s/he has won.
> The same applies in a war context (specifically here the Battle of Britain).

5. Explain the pun in the expression "bottle of Britain".

> 'Bottle of Britain' refers to the beer being advertised but *bottle* of course sounds very like *battle*. The advertisers are trying to link their product with nostalgic memories of WW2 among potential consumers.

6. What two things does the word "spitfire" refer to?

> The beer and the fighter plane.

7. What is the object in the bottom right-hand corner?

> It is the kind of pump used to serve draught beer.

8. Now you know how the advertisement is intended to be understood, how do you feel about it? Write a short personal comment.

> Students will know that the British tend to be obsessed by their successful role in WW2. They could be told that the Spitfire has been chosen as one of the ten most important British designs in recent years, more than 60 years after the war ended. Is it a good/tasteful idea to try and sell a beer on memories of the Battle of Britain so long after the event? It may help

to sell the beer – perhaps mainly to older customers or readers of some popular newspapers which keep plugging away at the Germans – but most reasonable people will regard it as witty but tasteless.

British-German relations – two views: Old enemies – new friends?

Questions to go with the photograph
1. Who are the three famous men in the photograph?
   (from left to right) Churchill, Roosevelt, Stalin (representing Britain, the US, Russia)
2. Why, in retrospect, is it quite surprising to see these three statesmen sitting together?
   Soon after the end of the war, the iron curtain came down and the cold war began, in which Russia and the West were on opposite sides.
3. Why might British people be rather fond of this photo?
   It shows the British leader (and greatest British citizen according to polls) as one of the 'big three' in the world. Britain's status in the world has declined in the following decades (loss of empire, economic problems, relative size, etc.).

Stop making fun of the hun
Catherine Mayer

The text
Attempts are being made in Britain to improve Germany's mainly war-based image in Britain. However, some Germans themselves remain obsessed by the war, which does not improve the situation. There is some support for the idea that Britain feels resentful about having 'lost the peace' while postwar Germany flourished. In the meantime more British people are taking flights to Germany to see the country for themselves. It is not clear that this will do very much to improve Germany's image in Britain. Some Britons are still hostile towards people with German accents, and do not want to admit to family links with Germany. America has a much more positive image, although this may have changed for the worse during the George W. Bush era.

Unterrichtsempfehlungen

Der kurze Autorentext „British-German relations, Old enemies – new friends"? ist eine gute Hinführung zum Haupttext „Stop making fun of the Hun", insbesondere für unsere Schüler/innen, die den Krieg und die Nachkriegszeit nicht miterlebt haben. Dazu trägt auch die Bildsequenz bei.

„Stop making fun of the Hun" ist sprachlich leicht zugänglich und kann ohne weitere Hilfen vorbereitet werden. Im dem sich anschließenden Klassengespräch werden die Schüler/innen zunächst ihre Eindrücke vom Text artikulieren und möglicherweise von dem berichten, was sie bisher über das Verhältnis zwischen Deutschland und Großbritannien von ihren Eltern gehört haben, und die Abbildungen kommentieren. Bei der Analyse des Textes von Catherine Mayer werden vermutlich folgende Aspekte genannt, die – mit Zitaten belegt – ausführlicher diskutiert werden müssen:

- Criticism of both sides
- slight improvement in British-German relations
- what still has to be done

Assignments – Solutions

1. Along what lines does Denis MacShane criticise both the British and the Germans?

> MacShane feels that politicians and people who form opinions in Britain know very little about Germany, and do hardly anything to put this right. He also feels that it is time for the Germans themselves to become less obsessed by the war.

2. How have British-German relations started to improve?

> More British people are travelling to Germany on cheap flights (but France remains far more popular, and very few of these visitors speak German).

3. And in what ways are they still far from perfect?

> Old stereotypes are still very much alive in Britain, although modern Germany is a very different place from Germany under Hitler. It seems as if Britain still needs to define itself as the country which beat Germany in the war (with a little help from her allies!).

4. How was the American author treated in an English school?

> There were some jokes at her expense about being a 'colonial', but other students were not really unfriendly.

5. Where does the author use 'warlike' language and images herself?

> - spearheading
> - laid down arms
> - leave the trenches
> - no man's land
> - won the war
> - lost the peace

6. How do you feel about this stylistic feature?

It adds interest to the article, but in a way she shares the very obsession she is complaining about.

7. Do you think the essay competition referred to at the beginning is a good idea? Give reasons for your answer.

Some ideas:
- Writing about (favourable) experiences can help to 'fix' them in the memory, so that the old views of Germany (reinforced by war films on TV and articles in the popular press) do not re-establish themselves once the visit is over.
- If other students read about positive experiences which their contemporaries have had in Germany, it can help to counterbalance the old stereotyped views.
- Unfortunately, the general effect of this competition is likely to be very small indeed.

8. Compare and contrast the attitudes referred to here with British attitudes to France.

British attitudes to:

Germany	France
Generally negative (with some recent improvements), linked to WW2, with Nazi stereotypes playing a major role. These views are reinforced by the popular media. They are firmly rooted in the past, and there is not enough first-hand experience of modem Germany to counteract them.	Very positive, linked with climate, life-style, food and drink (but not always with attitudes to French people, which may not be very favourable). The views relate mainly to present-day France, and are often based on personal experience.

9. Do you know the famous story behind the reference to a "kickabout in no man's land"? (l. 21)

On Christmas Day 1914 the soldiers in the trenches on the British and German sides had no wish to go on shelling one another. There were some exchanges of presents, food and drink, etc., some carol singing, and a game of football, England v. Germany, in no-man's land between the trenches. The result is not known. Apparently there was little wish to resume hostilities next day, and severe threats from senior officers on both sides were needed to get the war going again (some elements of this story may be apocryphal).

10. Can you explain the use of cockney rhyming slang in line 33f.?

In cockney slang a two-word expression which rhymes with the word in question is used instead of it. The link between the rhyming expression and the original word is often quite witty, e.g. Gawd (God) for<u>bids</u> = <u>kids</u>. Sometimes the actual rhyming word is left out, which makes the slang hard for outsiders to understand, e.g. "My plates are killing me" (plates of meat = feet). In the text example, septic tanks are used to store sewage in areas where there are no main drains, and of course they tend to be rather smelly, so this expression used for Americans is not exactly flattering.

11. A German student was working in a British comprehensive school a few years ago. The head teacher came into the room, and the form master introduced the student to him. The head teacher responded with a 'Hitler salute'. The student was shocked, but he managed to come up with a very effective reply. What would you have said?

The student could have replied along these lines:
Sir, I have to say that I am very shocked and upset to be greeted like that. I'm sure you meant it as a harmless joke, but it just isn't funny for us Germans. In fact this kind of salute is banned in Germany.

Kein Pardon. Der Queen-Besuch und das heikle deutsch-britische Verhältnis
Stefan Klein

The text
The author of the article begins by speculating humorously on items which the Queen might or might not bring with her on a recent visit to Germany. One thing which he does not think she will bring is an apology for the bombing of German cities in WW2. Worries about such matters show how tricky German-British relationships remain, with deep-seated prejudices, particularly on the British side, still very widespread. Fischer's* complaints about this state of affairs simply gave the popular media an opportunity to trot them all out again. There have even been complaints from the British side that the Germans are trying to airbrush unpleasant events from their history. Asking the Queen to apologise for the bombing is part of this trend. German institutions in Britain have tried to counteract the old clichés by means of a witty poster campaign making fun of them. This campaign seems to have had some success, but sending twenty English history teachers on a luxurious free trip to Germany looked a bit too much like bribery. The teachers seem to have found the trip embarrassing. It was unlikely that they would modify their teaching very much as a result of it.

The British Ambassador to Germany recently talked about the horrors of war, including the devastating firestorms caused by British bombing, but he did not apologise. The Queen will say all the right things, also including remarks about the horrors of war, but she will not apologise either.

---

* Fischer was the German foreign minister at the time.

Unterrichtsempfehlungen

Dass dieser der Süddeutschen Zeitung entnommene Artikel auf Deutsch abgedruckt ist, mag zunächst verwundern. Es entspricht jedoch der Realität, dass mündliche oder schriftliche Texte bei der Begegnung mit Ausländern ins Englische übertragen werden müssen. Den Schüler/innen wird hier die Möglichkeit geboten, sich in einer Art Simultanübersetzung zu üben (vgl. Aufgabe 1).

Der Artikel schließt sich unmittelbar an den vorangegangenen Text „Stop making fun of the Hun" an und beleuchtet das britisch-deutsche Verhältnis aus einer anderen Perspektive. Es geht um Klischees, die immer noch, insbesondere auf britischer Seite, festzustellen sind. Im Unterricht sollte daher das Hauptaugenmerk auf diese gelenkt werden.

Der Artikel wird nicht durch eine Frage-Antwort-Kette erschlossen, sondern *student-oriented*, d.h. selbstgesteuerte Entschlüsselung durch die Schüler/innen, möglichst verbunden mit deren Einschätzungen. Die Schülerbeiträge werden in einem entsprechend gestalteten *spidergram* an der Tafel festgehalten.

Board

```
British attitude ─┐           ┌─ German attitude
                  ┌─────────────────┐
                  │ British-German  │
                  │    relations    │
                  └─────────────────┘
students' comment ─┘           └─ students' comment
```

Assignments – Solutions

1. Imagine that a British exchange student who knows very little German sees the word 'Queen' in the title of this article, and asks what it is about. Explain in a short, informal summary.

> See the summary above.

2. Joschka Fischer obviously feels that 'mentioning the war' is Britain's problem, not Germany's. The popular press in Britain doesn't agree. Write a paragraph giving your own views – and try to suggest ways of improving the situation.

> Suggestions:
> - no doubt that the National Socialist period was Germany's blackest hour
> - understandable that Britain is proud of its role in defeating Hitler
> - but Nazi stereotypes persist although the war ended more than 60 years ago
> - need to find other, more favourable stereotypes – e.g. respected German farmers in the US during the main emigration period
> - no-one under 80 years of age in Germany can have been actively involved – possible that many British people do not realise this

- German cars very popular in Britain, Mercedes/BMW/Audi enjoying very high status. Perhaps some kind of charm offensive could be based on the car industry.

3. Compare the two articles about Britain and Germany. How far are the views expressed similar, and how do they differ?

Points to make:
- Both authors agree that British views of Germany are unfavourable.
- Both agree that attempts to improve matters have not generally been very successful.
- Both refer to the persistence of outdated Nazi stereotypes.
- Only Mayer refers to British resentment at Germany's success as a reason for British attitudes.
- Only Mayer compares attitudes to Germans with attitudes to Americans in Britain.
- Only Klein deals with the question of a British apology for the bombing of German cities.
- Only Klein deals with British teaching of German history.

Britain and Europe

Unterrichtsempfehlungen

Zu Beginn dieses Unterrichtsabschnitts wird für die mit der Entwicklung der EU vermutlich noch wenig vertrauten Schüler/innen anhand einer Europakarte und einer Übersicht über den historischen Weg zur EU (European milestones) ein Basiswissen vermittelt, das durch die Quizfragen noch gefestigt wird.

In einem historisch und politisch interessierten Kurs könnten die Informationen durch eine Internetrecherche vertieft werden.

Die letzte Frage des Aufgabenapparats leitet zum bereits in vorangegangenen Texten angesprochenen Verhältnis Großbritanniens zu Europa aus politischer Sicht mit einer Rede des Labour MEP (Member of the European Parliament) Gary Titley über: Only Labour values can take us forward in Europe.

Die Länge der Rede und die unterschiedlichsten Sachverhalte erschweren das Verständnis des Textes. Daher empfiehlt es sich, ihn in zwei Teilen zu behandeln. Die Rede kann entweder auditiv über Tonträger präsentiert oder lesend zur Kenntnis genommen werden. Die Zäsur sollte auf Seite 98, l. 65 erfolgen (bei *We have to:*). Nach der auditiven Präsentation bzw. dem individuellen Lesen der beiden Redeteile äußern die Schüler/innen zunächst spontan ihren Gesamteindruck. Vor der detaillierten Besprechung müssen die beiden Teile nochmals ein- bis zweimal studiert und mit Randnotizen (Blatt einlegen) versehen werden.

Die zu besprechenden Punkte werden von den Schülern zunächst ungeordnet an die Tafel geschrieben, evtl. durch den Lehrer ergänzt und schließlich in eine geeignete Chronologie gebracht. In der sich anschließenden detaillierten inhaltlichen Erschließung des Redetextes greifen die Schüler/innen auf ihre Notizen zurück. Die Analysepunkte werden stichwortartig an das Ende der jeweils abgehenden Linien geschrieben. Die Unterrichtsergebnisse sind eine gezielte Vorbereitung auf die schriftlich zu beantwortenden Fragen des Aufgabenapparats.

Map and verbal information, sample questions

- What is the capital of …
- What countries does (the Rhine) run through?
- Which European country has the largest/smallest area?
- Name some original/new members of the EU
- What was EFTA?
- What did the Schengen agreement lead to?
- Which countries are in the Eurozone?
- Name some countries on the waiting list to join.

Assignments – Solutions

1. List some advantages we enjoy as Europeans.

> Democratic government, high standard of living, no travel restrictions, good health services.

2. Does Europe have an 'Achilles heel' – or several?

> High rates of unemployment particularly for unskilled workers, low birth rates, rising health care costs, problems with financing pensions as people live longer, high energy costs

3. Can Europe compete with the US – or China?

> Europe may be able to compete if it concentrates on innovative products and high-status brands of all kinds, from cars to perfumes. However, China in particular is capable of making almost any product to increasingly high standards. America has problems of its own, with its motor industry in particular struggling to survive (uncompetitive products, pension costs).

4. Think of some issues on which Europeans from different countries disagree.

> Disagreement on attitudes to:
> - the common currency
> - immigrants
> - nuclear power
> - further integration
> - increasing power for 'Brussels' (interference in national affairs, loss of sovereignty)
> - market forces versus social democracy
> - defence policies

5. Why do you think Britain is often the odd man out?

> See the summary for Kaletzky's article, p. 99.

Only Labour values can take us forward in Europe
Gary Titley

Questions in the margin – Solutions

Examples of 'rubbishing' other parties
- the electorate got fed up with Michael Howard's opportunism … (l. 18 f.)
- (the Liberals) wallowed in the tragedies of Iraq … (l. 37)
- the UK Independence Party – the BNP with suits and posh accents (l. 40)
  … paranoid, obsessive, little Englanders … grumpy old men.
- blatant racism from some parties (l. 118)

How does Titley deal with his disappointment over the election result?

> He points out that all governing parties did badly in the election, but only in Britain did the main opposition party also lose seats.

What exactly is the new 'divide' which Titley refers to here?

> It is between those who want to see Britain embracing globalisation/playing its full part on the international stage and those who are in favour of a 'little Britain' policy, which means a return to insularity and anti-immigration laws.

The text
(1. Thanking party workers and candidates)
The author, Gary Titley, begins by thanking everyone who worked in the European Election campaign, and goes on to praise the high quality of the candidates.
(2. Attacking the Conservatives)
However, the results were disappointing for Labour, as they were for other government parties across Europe, but in Britain there were no corresponding gains for the Conservative opposition. He accuses their leader at the time of changing his mind again and again, which resulted in their worst election result since 1832.
(3. Attacking the Liberals and the UKIP)
The liberals were no better, while the UKIP, who did make some gains, was a party of grumpy old men stuck in the past. They claimed to be patriotic, but they supported Paris for the 2012 Olympics, and cannot be taken seriously as members of the European Parliament.
(4. Praising the European Parliament)
Titley sees the European Parliament as an exciting Organisation, with people from the new member states of the EU bringing in fresh, optimistic ways of thinking. All its members are determined to lead the way in finding solutions to Europe's problems.

(5. Tasks for the European Parliament)
A list of problems which the EU has to tackle comes next. It includes issues such as jobs, the environment, world trade, crime and terrorism.
(6. The need for a European Constitution)
Ratifying the European Constitution would be a good way to start.
(7. Recent achievements)
Titley guarantees that the European Labour party will be working hard on all these issues in the future. He demonstrates its effectiveness by listing some progress his party has already achieved. It includes measures designed to help handicapped people, protect air travellers, the victims of domestic crime and dolphins, and fight various kinds of crime. He is proud of this record.
(8. Britain's role in a globalised world)
He is nevertheless very worried that half the British people who voted in the European elections voted for anti-European parties. The country is split between those who want to grasp the opportunities of globalisation, and those who simply wish it would go away. He sees his own party as firmly on the side of change. The case for reform must be made with strength and conviction at every opportunity.
(9. Conclusion: winning the battle for Britain and Europe)
If Britain does not succeed in changing in a changing world, the future is black. The country will be destroyed if those who are against everything foreign gain the upper hand. The battle must be won by Labour, the party which believes in prosperity, freedom and opportunity in a European context.

Board: Geordnetes Tafelbild und erwartetes Ergebnis des Unterrichtsgesprächs

Titley's speech

Parties ↓

Attacking the Conservatives	– only opposition party to lose
	– fed up with Howard's opportunism
	– fed up with flip-flops
	– fed up with contradictions
Attacking the Liberals and the UKIP	Liberals
	– inconsistent
	– did not mention Europe
	– exploited Iraq war
	UKIP
	– right-wing party
	– anti immigration/EU
	– out of date
	– sexist
Censuring people who voted for anti-Euopean parties	– want the rest of the world to go away
	– against foreigners/immigration
	– racist
	– a national disgrace

Only Labour values can take us forward in Europe 113

Achievements of the EPLP	– city buses with disability access
	– investment in infrastructure projects
	– funding to fight domestic violence
European Parliament ↓	
Praising the European Parliament	– vibrant and exciting
	– MEP's from the new member states bring in new ideas and attitudes
	– want Europe to work
	– all EPLP members prepared to work hard for success
Tasks for the European Parliament	(for Titley these are the same as the aims for the EPLP)
	– New and better jobs
	– a more dynamic economy
	– environmental protection
	– coordinated response to world crises
	– fair trade
	– better laws
	– effective action against crime and terrorism
The need for a European Constitution	– should be ratified
	– without it, the EU will not be able to respond to challenges

Assignments – Solutions

1. (Titley's) speech has a number of different sections. Try to decide where these sections begin and end, and give each of them a title.

Parts of Titley's speech with titles:
1. (ll. 1–13) thanking party workers and candidates
2. (ll. 14–33) Attacking the Conservatives
3. (ll. 34–52) Attacking the liberals and the UKIP
4. (ll. 53–64) Praising the European Parliament
5. (ll. 65–73) Tasks for the European Parliament
6. (ll. 74–78) The need for a European constitution
7. (ll. 79–90 (91)) Recent achievements
8. (ll. 92–117) Britain's role in a globalised world
9. (ll. 118–120) The dangers/disgrace of discrimination and racism
10. (ll. 121–125) Conclusion: winning the battle for Britain and Europe

2. Write an integrated paragraph which includes a sentence or two about each section.

See the summary above.

3. The last paragraph refers to a "battle" about the future of Britain and Europe. What European issues are people arguing about at the moment?

Current issues:
unemployment, enlargement, immigration, interest rates, foreign policies, particularly in connection with Iraq, Iran

4. Analyse the speech (structural and rhetorical devices). Find examples for the aspects referred to in the information box on page 96.

One-sided: Titley is pro Labour and against all other parties throughout.
Attacking other parties: See the notes on rubbishing other parties above.
Emotional language: government parties got hammered (l. 14f.)
fed up with his flip-flops (l. 19)
wallowed in the tragedies of Iraq (l. 37)
paranoid, obsessive ... backwoods-men (ll. 42–43)
vibrant and exciting (l. 53)
...
Structural devices: repeated structures, e.g. 'One moment' repeated 4 times (several other examples)
Lists: e.g. We have to: create new and better jobs
                          make Europe's economy more dynamic
Addressing the audience directly:
                          use of the term CONFERENCE

5. Political speeches tend to be very one-sided, but at least in a democracy other parties are free to express *their* views with just as much bias and enthusiasm.

a) Is an adversarial culture the price we have to pay for living in a democracy?
b) On the other hand, democratic systems have to aim at a consensus on important issues. Does this process take up too much time and energy?
c) What happens to freedom of speech in non-democratic systems?
d) Is there anything to be said in favour of such systems?

Personal opinion but here are some brief thoughts:
a) It seems to be – the alternative is a one-party system.
b) It does take up a great deal of time – see any attempt in Germany to enlarge airports, for example.
c) Freedom of speech is systematically suppressed, journalists and editors are threatened (sometimes even murdered), or have their newspapers closed down. Only the 'official' view is available via the media.
d) Sometimes the view is expressed that one-party systems are better at 'getting things done' – because the opposition is powerless to stop what the government wants to do – good or bad.
But: 'Absolute power corrupts absolutely' (attributed to Lord Acton).

6. Now it's your turn. Think of an issue which you feel strongly about and write a speech supporting your views. Use some of the devices referred to above, and try to make it really convincing. Practise reading it aloud, and try it out on your fellow students.

Creative writing/delivering a speech

Does Britain need Europe?

What does the expression 'top dog' mean?
The person or country which is, or thinks it is superior to others, and enjoys various advantages as a result (cf. modern terms such as *alpha male*).
Each of the three largest countries in the EU is represented by a 'typical' dog according to common stereotypes/clichés (France: a poodle, Germany: a dachshund, sometimes called a German sausage dog) and Britain: a bulldog. The three dogs have taken part in a dog show, where rosettes are awarded for first, second and third prize.

Unterrichtsempfehlungen

Der kurze Text, das diesem zuzuordnende Bild und die Grafiken beleuchten das bisher gewonnene Bild Großbritanniens im neuen Europa aus einer anderen, u. a. wirtschaftlichen Perspektive. Die Informationen werden durch Grafiken vermittelt, die zum Darstellungsmedium jeder Zeitung und jedes Fachaufsatzes gehören und auch in Oberstufenmaterialien für den Englischunterricht einen Platz haben.
Die Schüler sollten zur Analyse der auf den Seiten 101 und 102 abgedruckten vier (unterschiedlichen) Grafiken eine Kopie des folgenden Analyserasters, erhalten.

> **Working with graphs – How to proceed**
> 1. Orientation
>   - What type of graph is presented and what is its subject?
>   - What is the source of the graph, and is it still topical?
> 2. Description
>   - Describe the graph.
>   - Analyse it (developments, peaks/low points, etc.).
> 3. Evaluation
>   - Do you think the graph is authentic or does it try to manipulate people?

Working with graphs
You can interpret the graphs quite easily with the help of the expressions given below.
a) The first graph compares economic growth in Britain with that in the Euro area/zone.
   It covers the period from 1994–2000.

It demonstrates that, according to this criterion, Britain has been considerably more successful than the Eurozone during this period.
unemployment (second graph)
1994-2004
Britain has been more successful at dealing with unemployment than the Eurozone.

b) pie chart:
This pie chart deals with voting intentions if there was a referendum on the EU constitution. Voters were asked how they would vote on this issue.
Only 23 % were in favour at the time. The largest group would vote against.
Quite large percentages were 'don't knows', would not vote, or said they would decide nearer the time.

c) bar graph:
People felt most strongly about the power to decide tax rates for their own country.
They also felt it was important to retain UK policy on asylum seekers.
Just over half wanted to keep the pound
About a third wanted to retain UK decision-making on military action and on the right to leave the EU.

Assignments – Solutions

1. When you have talked about the four graphs, write a short essay comparing Britain with the rest of Europe. If you feel that things have changed since these voters were consulted, be sure to say so, with evidence to back up your view if possible. Bring in material from other parts of the unit as appropriate.

> The whole unit can be seen as preparation for this activity.

2. Write a dialogue between yourself and a fairly patriotic English student you could meet on holiday in Germany, Britain or elsewhere. Read the dialogue out to the class with a partner.

> The dialogue could begin as follows:
>
> (somewhere in the South of France)
>
> German student: On holiday here?
> English student: Yes. Great weather. You too?
> G: Just down for a few days – I've got to get back for my exams.
> E: Tough! I'm just going to lie in the sun for a few weeks
> G: Nice. Did you come down by car?
> E: Yes – that's my Toyota over there?
> G: Not very patriotic of you to buy a Toyota.
> E: Well, at least it's reliable.
> G: Not like Rovers, you mean.
> E: Hang on now.
> G: …

The British-American 'party'
Jeremy Paxman

Whatever the economic imbalance (after the Second World War), the British convinced themselves that they brought something special to the party ...
In the longer term, the (British-American) alliance enabled the British to delude themselves that they remained an independent power in the world. Characteristically, what the British had seen as 'independence' was merely independence from the rest of Europe. The relationship with the United States was merely one of being free to do as they pleased, as long as Washington did not object, as the British discovered in 1956 when they tried to invade Egypt to secure the Suez Canal, without American approval. But by then, the die was cast; Britain had thrown in her lot with what was seen as a kindred Anglo-Saxon culture across the Atlantic. In the context of British history it was understandable: Europe meant war, America the aid which ended war. But the price of British overdependence on the United States was that the country closed its eyes to much else happening in Europe and aggravated its estrangement from the European Community to which, belatedly, it sought admission. It has never caught up since. By the 1990s, with the continent of Europe no longer divided between communism and democracy, when the 'Special Relationship' with Britain mattered a great deal less to the United States, it was left blowing in the wind.
The relationship with the United States is still 'special'. It shows in the curious personal friendships which can develop between political leaders who literally as well as metaphorically speak the same language – Thatcher and Reagan, or Blair and Clinton. While Harold Wilson successfully kept Britain out of the Vietnam debacle, in other postwar conflicts, from Korea to Kosovo, British governments pride themselves on their readiness to send forces to fight alongside (for) America. It shows in the vast British investment in the United States (greater than that of any other European country); in the fact that there is more American investment in Britain than in any other European country, in the interpenetration of British and American cinema, where a certain kind of villain always has an English accent; in the English-Speaking Union, the Atlantic Council and dozens of other clubs; and in the fact that more than twice as many people travel between Britain and North America as cross the Atlantic to or from any other European state. Indeed, you need to add together all the travellers from Germany, France and the Netherlands to North America, to exceed the British people travelling.

Klausurvorschlag

The comparison with ancient Greece and Rome is made less frequently now, as it becomes clearer than ever to the English that the world is Made in America. How do you explain to a country dressed in jeans, T-shirts and baseball caps that they belong to a culture which gave the world that universal item of clothes, the tailored man's suit? You don't. It doesn't matter any more.

(375 words)

Assignments

1. Why was it a delusion for the British to think they were still an independent power after the Second World War?
2. What negative consequences did overdependence on the United States have?
3. In what ways is Britain's relationship with the US still 'special', and how does Paxman introduce his evidence for this special relationship?
4. Can you explain the following figurative expressions:
   a) the die was cast (l. 11)
   b) to throw in one's lot (l. 12)
   c) blowing in the wind (l. 21)
   d) metaphorically speak the same language (l. 24)
5. How far do you accept the view that the modern world is 'Made in America'?
6. On the whole Germany seems to be more pro-Europe and less pro-America than Britain. Write a paragraph explaining why this may be the case, making use of material from the unit and from recent news items.

Solutions

1. Britain could not in fact do anything on an international scale without American support. When Britain tried to invade Egypt without America, the operation failed. Britain was no longer the powerful nation she had been during the colonial period.

2. Negative consequences:
- little knowledge/understanding of what was going on across the Channel
- estrangement from the European Community
- joined belatedly and has remained to some extent on the fringes of the EU
- when ex-communist countries became part of 'Europe' again after the end of communism, Britain was still looking to America, which wasn't very interested in Britain.

3. Relationship still special:
- personal transatlantic friendships between top people
- British support for American military activities as a rule
- large American investments in Britain
- links via the cinema
- clubs linking members in both countries
- travel

These points are introduced by a series of statements introduced by *it shows ...*

4. a) no further change was possible (metaphor from casting in metal – a die is a tool or mould used for producing a series of identical items)
b) to share one's fate with someone else
c) abandoned and useless (cf. the famous Bob Dylan song: "The answer, my friend, is blowing in the wind ...")
d) a lot of common ground/cultural similarities/historical links/shared assumptions

5. Some points which could be made:
- English is the international language/main Internet language.
- America is the only remaining superpower.
- American fashions adopted all over the (non-Muslim) world.
- American innovation/dominance in many areas (computers, aviation, Nobel prize-winners)

Possible to argue on the other side of the case that American dominance is gradually coming to an end – expensive oil, rise of India/China, difficulties with financing its very expensive way of life/huge consumption of natural resources

6. Pro-Europe
- on the mainland/at the heart of Europe
- founder member of the European Community/always an insider
- largest member in terms of population/economic power
- after the war Germany was happy to be part of a larger grouping (German nationalism discredited)
- belief in European ideas and ideals

Anti-America
- against American military adventures (anti-war for obvious reasons)
- (slightly) less ready to adopt unhealthy American fast food
- dislike of President George W. Bush and his policies
- some envy of America's global success in many fields
- poor social services for poor people

The question of Britishness that even had the Palace stumped

By Richard Ford

Home Correspondent

The question of who is the head of the Church of England produced much head-scratching at Buckingham Palace the headquarters of the Church and Lambeth Palace, official residence of the Archbishop of Canterbury.

Buckingham Palace and the Church of England were at one. "Christ is head," spokesmen for both the Church and monarch said. The Palace was confident. "Christ is head of the Church of England, um, the Queen is, um, let me look … Defender of the Faith and Supreme Governor," it said.

The Church of England said: "Christ is head, while head of the Church is the Sovereign, she is Supreme Governor. She is the source of all legal authority."

If that isn't clear enough, Lambeth Palace had a different interpretation. "Let me get the wording right, the Archbishop is the spiritual head of the Church of England," it said.

Foreigners wishing to become British citizens will have to answer such as this to pass a "life in Britain" test. This particular question has been dropped after the Home Office document on which the test is based described the Queen and the Archbishop of Canterbury as "head of the Church".

Teachers complained yesterday that the test would be too difficult for many people born here, and on the above evidence, they might have a point.

Thousands of immigrants will have to take the new test from today, though those with very poor English will have to show only that they have improved their language skills.

Tony McNulty, the Immigration Minister, promised that the new tests would not be so "rigorous" as to deter immigrants from seeking to become citizens. He also told a conference in London that the testing regime would be extended to those who wish only to settle in the country rather than acquire a British passport.

Foreigners who speak English fluently will be tested on their knowledge of life in Britain, its customs and culture. Those with language skills below fluency will be tested on their command of English.

Applicants for citizenship will have to produce a certificate showing that they have passed the Life in UK test or one indicating that they passed a test in proficiency in English. They must then attend citizenship ceremonies. It is only after making an oath of allegiance to the Queen and a pledge of loyalty to Britain that citizenship is awarded.

People wishing to acquire a British passport will pay £34 to sit a 45-minute online exam. They must answer correctly 75 per cent of the 24 multiple-choice questions before being awarded a certificate.

The website makes clear that the object is to help people to integrate into Britain rather than testing to fail a specific percentage of applicants.

However, one teacher of English has asked whether similar tests would be imposed on existing citizens. Connie Hancock, from the University of Chester, said that though she had two degrees she was not sure how to answer a question about which courts had juries. In a test among trainers involved in the scheme, only one out of 20 had passed, she said.

(The Times, Tuesday November 1, 2005)

Additional text

The UK entry quiz

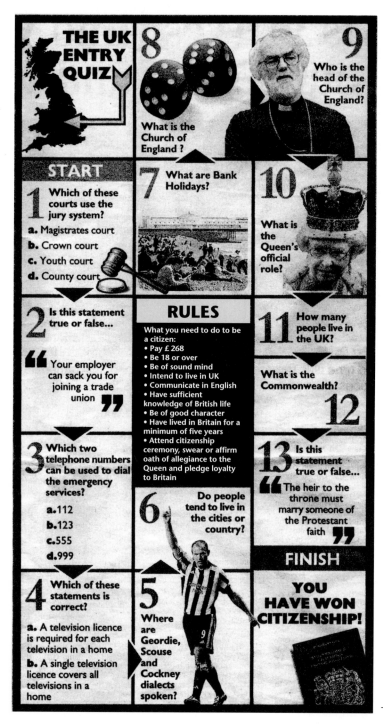

The Times, November 1, 2005

Solutions

1) b

2) False

3) 112 and 999

4) b

5) Tyneside, Liverpool, London

6) Cities

7) When by law banks must close

8) The established church of England

9) The Archbishop of Canterbury

10) Head of State of the United Kingdom

11) 58.8 million

12) An association of largely independent states that formed the British Empire

13) True

Ask the people

The Times asked members of the public questions typical of those in the Life in the UK test. Only one out of seven people asked got all four questions right.

Spencer Coleman 53, art shop owner from Louth, Lincolnshire – three correct: "I would have thought most people should be expected to know members of the monarchy and the Government. You should be aware that someone like William Shakespeare was born in England."

Tanya Abraham 40, librarian, Muswell Hill, London – two correct: "I don't see how any of those denotes Britishness. It's your commitment to the place where you live that makes you a citizen, if you're going to uphold the law of the land, pay your taxes and take responsibility and vote."

Usman Malik 35, telecoms engineer, Hayes, West London – all four correct: "I've recently got British citizenship and I wouldn't have minded if I got questions like that. I'm from Pakistan and I've lived here for six years. As long as I feel this is my home, that's Britishness to me."

(The Times, Tuesday November 1, 2005)

Europe old and young
Stephen Speight

A French student (François) and a German student (Gabi) are sitting in a pub, talking about their experiences during an exchange scheme with an English university. An OAP at the next table is listening to their conversation.

F: Another drink, Gabi?
G: No thanks, François – I can't drink as much as these English students do – Germans are supposed to drink a lot, but the Brits drink more!
F: You're telling me! I've had a really good term here though.
G: Me, too. Did you get to see a bit of the countryside?
F: Not really. My business studies course kept me pretty busy.
G: I'm doing EFL, as you know. The staff took us on some nice trips. But I wish I'd had a car with me.
F: Would you have been happy driving on the wrong side of the road?
O: Just a second, young feller. Just because we drive on the left, it doesn't mean it's the wrong side! We think the left side is the *right* side!
F: OK. Sorry! But you must admit that driving on the *other* side is a bit difficult for us foreigners.
G: I can't understand why Britain doesn't change over.
O: Why should we? The Japanese drive on the left, and the Indians I think – that's quite a lot of people who drive on our side of the road!
G: Ah – but they're a long way from Europe!

Additional text

O: What's Europe got to do with it?

F: Well your country **is** in the EU isn't it?

O: We may be in the EU, but we're not really *in* Europe, are we. For us, Europe is foreign.

G: Well, we **could** say that Britain is foreign for us, but it doesn't really seem like that – we speak your language for a start.

O: Yes, we're lucky there – English kids don't really need to learn foreign languages – everybody speaks ours.

F: I think English kids are **un**lucky. Everybody should speak two or three languages.

O: Why? I'm quite happy with one – and so was Shakespeare. And while I'm at it, there's nothing wrong with the pound sterling or the way we run things generally, thank you very much!

F: We don't want to argue with you. We like Britain, too. But when I had toothache, it was really difficult to get an appointment at the dentist's.

G: And when we went on a trip to the Lake District, we drove through some really awful towns.

O: Well, I'm not saying everything's perfect. My pension, for a start!

F: Oh – let me get you another beer, sir.

O: Thank you. I won't say no to that! *(F goes over to the bar)*

G: I hope you don't mind me asking – were you in the war?

O: Yes, I went over to France on D-Day. Terrible times. Later I saw what your cities looked like after the bombing – you are German, aren't you?

G: Yes. I suppose my accent still gives me away.

O: Don't worry about that. Your English is excellent – just sounds a bit different. We were rather envious of the way you rebuilt everything and got your industry going after the war.

G: But now Britain seems to be very successful – at least, that's what it says in the newspapers.

O: Successful for some – businessmen, footballers and pop stars.

G: But the middle classes seem to be doing all right too – they're all making money on their houses.

O: Seems like it. But plenty of people aren't on the bandwagon like in those northern towns you saw.

F: *(returns with drinks for everyone)* Santé!

G: Prost!

O: Cheers!

G: I think all our countries have plenty to offer – we make good cars –

F: And we have the best trains, wine, countryside, climate, coast …

O: Hey, I can't agree with all of that!

G: Nor me. What about the Rhine, the Baltic Coast … What about Paris?

G: We've got **lots** of really great cities, too, Berlin, Hamburg, Munich, Cologne …

F: And I'd like to know what you actually make in Britain nowadays. Your last big home-owned car company went bust!

O: You're right about that. I'm a bit of a car freak, and that really hurt, I can tell you. But this is still a great place to live.

F and G: We'll drink to that – Cheers!

Reel or real? – A television series

Funktion und Aufbau des Kapitels

Ein Ziel des Englischunterrichts der Sekundarstufe II ist der Aufbau einer Medienkompetenz (*media literacy*), d.h. der Fähigkeit, das breite Medienangebot mündig und kritisch nutzen zu können. Der Umgang mit audiovisuellen Medien wird in *People Around You* anhand der ersten Folge der amerikanischen Fernsehserie *Dawson's Creek* eingeübt. Sie hat den Titel *Emotions in Motion (pilot)*. Da sie einen Umfang von ca. 40 Minuten Länge hat, kann sie auch bei knapper Unterrichtszeit ganz gesehen und als Einheit behandelt werden.

Die Einstiegsseite mit den Bildern aus verschiedenen Fernsehserien (von denen jeweils zwei zum selben Format gehören) bietet den Schülern die Möglichkeit, ihr Vorwissen zu artikulieren und die unterschiedlichen Kategorien von Fernsehprogrammen (Formaten) zu erkennen und zu benennen.

Nach einem kurzen Überblick über den *process of filmmaking* sollen die Schüler am Beispiel dieser Folge von *Dawson's Creek* schrittweise mit filmischen Mitteln und deren Wirkungsweise vertraut gemacht werden. Ziel ist es, die Schüler zu befähigen, zunächst eine Sequenz der Serie, letztendlich aber jede Filmszene und ganze Filme selbstständig und selbstverantwortlich zu analysieren und zu bewerten.

Grundlegend für die Filmanalyse ist das Erkennen, Benennen und Interpretieren der vom Regisseur geplanten und von Filmtechnikern und Schauspielern umgesetzten filmischen Gestaltungsmittel, die vom Zuschauer über die beiden Kanäle „Sehen" und „Hören" wahrgenommen werden. Wichtig ist hierbei, die Schüler für die Interdependenz von Inhalt und Form des Films zu sensibilisieren, d.h. die erkannten *cinematic devices* müssen in Beziehung zu der inhaltlichen Aussage gebracht werden. Diese Vorgehensweise ist den Schülern im Grunde genommen von der Textarbeit bekannt.

Natürlich muss sich eine Einführung in die Filmanalyse in der gymnasialen Oberstufe auf die Vermittlung einer grundlegenden, schulisch sinnvollen Terminologie beschränken. In diesem Sinn ermöglicht dieses Kapitel eine schrittweise und systematische Erschließung v.a. folgender Elemente des Films und deren Funktion:

- pre-credit sequence
- credit sequence
- subtext
- field size, camera range (Einstellungsgröße)
- cinematic point-of-view (Darstellungsperspektive)
- camera angle (Kameraperspektive)
- camera movement (Kamerabewegung)
- punctuation (Übergänge)

- editing (Montage)
- light, colour (Licht, Farbe)
- sound (Ton)
- dialogue (Sprache, Text)

Bei der Einführung der Darstellungsperspektive (*cinematic point-of-view*, Schülerbuch S. 114) werden die Schüler aufgefordert, sich ein eigenes, persönliches Glossar zur Filmterminologie anzulegen, das im weiteren Verlauf der Unterrichtsreihe immer wieder ergänzt wird (*mini projects*). Da viele Begriffe der Filmsprache durch entsprechende Bilder sehr viel leichter zu erfassen sind und die Suche nach geeigneten Bildern den Verstehensprozess der Schüler unterstützt, ist das Ergänzen der im *glossary of film terms* (Schülerbuch S. 126) gegebenen Definitionen durch passende Bilder eine gewinnbringende Aufgabe mit anschaulichem Ergebnis, auf das die Schüler bis zum Abitur immer wieder zurückgreifen können.

Im Anschluss an die Untersuchung der Folge von *Dawson's Creek* sollen die Schüler mit der Textsorte Filmkritik (*film review*) vertraut gemacht werden, indem sie anhand einer Kritik zu dem Film *Clueless* die einzelnen Elemente und deren Anordnung im Text aufdecken. Schließlich sollen die Schüler ihr erworbenes Wissen anwenden, indem sie selbst eine Kritik zu der untersuchten Folge von *Dawson's Creek* und einem Film ihrer Wahl verfassen.

Literaturhinweise

Boggs, Joseph M./Petrie, Dennis W.: The Art of Watching Film. Sixth edition. Mayfield Publishing Company. Mountain View, California 2004

Hickethier, Knut: Film- und Fernsehanalyse. Stuttgart: Melzer 2001

Hildebrand, Jens: Film. Ratgeber für Lehrer. Köln: Aulis Verlag Deubner & Co. KG 2001

Kamp, W./Rüsel, M.: Vom Umgang mit … Film. Berlin: Volk und Wissen 1998

Liebelt, W.: „Anregungen für den Umgang mit Video im Fremdsprachenunterricht." In: PRAXIS des neusprachlichen Unterrichts. Heft 3, 1989

ders.: The Language of Film; Tipps für die Medienpraxis Nr. 6, Hannover NLI o. J.

Monaco, James: How to read a Film. The World of Movies, Media, Multimedia: Language, History, Theory. USA: Oxford: Oxford University Press. 3rd edition 2000

Sommer, Roy/Zerweck, Bruno: „TV Literacy in der Fernsehgesellschaft". In: Der Fremdsprachliche Unterricht English 75, 2005, S. 2–9

Stempelski, Susan/Tomalin, Barry: Film. Resource Books for Teachers. Oxford: Oxford University Press 2001

Thaler, Engelbert: „Methoden zur Arbeit mit TV-Sitcoms". In: Der Fremdsprachliche Unterricht 75, 2005, S. 36–37

Introduction

Die Bilder der Einstiegsseite (Schülerbuch S. 107) dienen dazu, die Schüler im Sinne einer *previewing activity* dazu anzuregen, über die Fernsehprogramme zu sprechen und die Begriffe *Genre* und *Format* einzuführen. Im Gespräch über die durch Bilder repräsentierten Fernsehserien werden die Schüler herausfinden, dass jeweils zwei zusammengehören, da sie demselben Format angehören. Es kann davon ausgegangen werden, dass die Schüler mit den meisten Programmen und einigen Formaten sowie mit dem Begriff *Genre* vertraut sind. Wahrscheinlich muss der Begriff *Format (format)* aber vom Lehrer eingeführt werden.

In pairs or small groups, try to find links between the following pictures from TV programmes, group them into pairs and name them. Explain your decision.

Solution

number	name of the programme	format
1	Friends	comedy
8	Sex and the City	comedy
2	Dark Angel	science fiction
12	Star Trek	science fiction
4	Sponge Bob	cartoon
10	The Simpsons	cartoon
5	The O. C.	drama
3	Gilmore Girls	drama
6	Relic Hunter	action/adventure
11	V.I.P.	action/adventure
7	The Osbournes	reality
9	The Simple Life	reality

Bevor man mit der Analyse von *Dawson's Creek* beginnt, ist es sinnvoll, grundlegende Informationen zum Entstehungsprozess eines Films zu sichern, wie sie der Text im Schülerbuch auf Seite 108 liefert. Die folgende Aufgabe beabsichtigt, den Schülern die Namen und Funktionen der an einem Film beteiligten Personen in Erinnerung zu bringen und darüber zu sprechen, indem sie die Begriffe ihren Definitionen zuordnen.
Diese Aufgabe kann in Partner- oder Kleingruppenarbeit gelöst werden. Die Sicherung der Ergebnisse könnte in der Form geschehen, das ein Schüler eine Definition vorliest und ein anderer Schüler den gesuchten Bebriff nennt.

Match the following terms with their corresponding definitions and make a list of the most important people and their function in the production of a film.

Solution:

| 1-e | 3-g | 5-a | 7-k | 9-f | 11-d |
| 2-l | 4-i | 6-m | 8-c | 10-b | 12-h |

Dawson's Creek – a very popular drama

Writer, director, cast of the first TV episode

Studio: Columbia Tristar

Rating: NR (not rated)

Writer/creator: Kevin Williamson, born 1965 in New Bern, North Carolina, USA, is a **screenplay writer** (e.g. *Glory Days* (TV series 2002), *Scream 1–3* (1996, 1997, 2000), *The Faculty* (1998), *I Know What You Did Last Summer* (1997)), **producer** (e.g. *Cursed* (2005), *Glory Days* (TV series 2002), *Scream* (1997)), **actor** (e.g. *Scream 2* (1997), *Hot Ticket* (1996), *Another World* (TV series 1964)) and **director** (*Teaching Mrs Tingle* (1999).

Director: Steve Miner, born 1951 in Westport, Connecticut, USA, is the **director** of numerous TV series and episodes (e.g. *Wildfire* (2005), *North Shore* (2004), *Karen Sisco* (2003), *Smallville* (2002), *Texas Rangers* (2001), *Chicago Hope* (1994), *Friday the 13th, part 2* (1981), **producer** (e.g. *Warlock* (1989), *The Wonder Years* (1988), *Manny's Orphans* (1978)) and **actor** (e.g. *Lake Placid* (1999), *Halloween H20:20 Years Later* (1998)).

Cast:
Dawson Leery: James Van Der Beek (born 1977 in Cheshire, Connecticut, USA).
Filmography: *The Plague* (2006), *Three* (TV series 2005), *Scary Movie* (2000), *Varsity Blues* (1999), *I Love You, I Love You Not* (1996)
Josephine Potter (Joey): Katie Holmes (born 1978 in Toledo, Ohio, USA)
Filmography: *Batman Begins* (2005), *First Daughter* (2004), *Phone Booth* (2002), *Wonder Boys* (2002), *The Ice Storm* (1997)
Jennifer Lindly (Jen): Michelle Williams (born 1980 in Kalispell, Montana, USA).
Filmography: *Brokeback Mountain* (2006), *The Hawk Is Dying* (2006), *The Baxter* (2005), *Land Of Plenty* (2004), *Prozak Nation* (2001), *Species* (1995)
Pacey Whitter: Joshua Jackson (born 1978 in Vancouver, British Columbia, Canada)
Filmography: *Bobby* (2006), *Cursed* (2005), *I Love Your Work* (2003), *Gossip* (2000), *Urban Legend* (1998), *Scream* (1997).

The series: *Dawson's Creek* is a very successful American dramatic series that consists of 128 episodes (six seasons) which were first shown in the USA from 1998 to 2003. (The first season was released on DVD on April 1, 2003). It is also popular in European countries including the United Kingdom, Germany, Italy, Sweden, France, Hungary and Spain, as well as in Australia, New Zealand, Israel and Brazil. By the end of its run the series had been nominated for fourteen awards, winning four.

year	award	category/recipient	result
2004	Golden Satellite Award	Best DVD Release of TV Shows	nominated
2003	TV Guide Award	Favorite Teen Show	nominated
2001	Teen Choice Award	TV-Choice Actor: Joshua Jackson	won
2000	GLAAD Media Award	Outstanding TV Drama Series	won

1999	Teen Choice Award	TV-Choice Actor: Joshua Jackson	won
		TV-Choice Drama	won
		TV-Choice Actress: Katie Holmes	nominated
1998	Young Star Award	Best Performance by a young Actress in a Drama TV Series: Michelle Williams	nominated

Dawson's Creek is set in the fictional small seaside town of Capeside, Massachusetts in the late 90's and aimed at teenagers since it focuses on the lives of four teenagers and the issues they have to face on their passage from adolescence to young adulthood.
More information can be found on the internet:
www.dawsonscreek.com (official site)
www.imdb.com (basic information and numerous links)
www.angelfire.com/ks/deskrits/100.html (script)

Szenenprotokoll Dawson's Creek, episode 1: "Emotions in Motion"

scene	content	running time
pre-credit	Dawson's room at night: Dawson and Joey are watching a movie; she wants to leave, but he is able to persuade her to spend the night (as usual)	00:00
opening credits	introduction of the main characters (Dawson, Joey, Paycey, Jen) and the setting Capeside: (sailing boats, docks)	03:15
1	morning at the docks: Dawson is filming a scene for the movie he wants to present at a festival: Pacey and Joey are acting	04:20
2	Jen, the new girl from New York arrives in a cab; they introduce themselves	05:05
3	Dawson's house: Dawson and Pacey find his parents kissing in the living room	06:30
4	Joey's house: her sister's boyfriend lets her taste a sauce he made; she has a little argument with her pregnant sister about tidying up her room	07:18
5	at the video store: Dawson and Pacey are working after school	08:12

6	Nellie, the store owner's daughter teases Pacey	08:25
7	a beautiful woman, Tamara Jacobs, enters the store. She flirts with Pacey and rents the video of *The Graduate*. He is very impressed.	09:20
8	dock in front of Dawson's house: Dawson spots Jen sitting alone on the dock. They talk about his passion for film, he shows her his "studio"	11:13
9	Dawson's house: Joey starts to climb the ladder to his room, but pauses at the top when she hears voices. She waits until Jen leaves (her grandma calls her), then gets into Dawson's room through the window	13:15
10	Dawson and Joey watch Dawson's mom read the news on TV, Dawson thinks his mom might be having an affair with her coanchor	14:12
11	morning, Jen's house: she talks to her unconscious granddad	14:55
12	Grams prepares breakfast, she tells Jen not to join Dawson and Joey because they are "the wrong element"; they have a dicusssion about religion	16:02
13	Capeside Highschool: students arriving, playing, talking in front of the school; hall: Jen meets Nellie Olsen	17:35
14	Dawson arrives, he walks to her biology class	18:38
15	classroom: Pacey learns that the woman from the video store is his new English teacher; biology room: Jen takes a seat next to Joey (who is not very pleased to see her)	19:03
16	another classroom: Dawson talks to the teacher of the film class because he was denied admittance	19:48
17	hall: Jen and Joey walk out of Biology, Jen asks Joey whether she and Dawson are a pair, she replies that they are just friends; Joey explains why Jen's grandma does not like her family and tells her that Dawson likes her; she asks her not to abuse his feelings	21:33
18	school cafeteria: Dawson, Joey and Jen talk about teachers; Dawson finds Jen funny and wants her to help him with the dialogue for his script; Joey wants to leave with him	22:29
19	teachers' room: Pacey offers to make a reservation for a video for Tamara, but she tells him she wants to go to the movies that night; he says he might go, too	23:03
20	hall: Pacey tells Dawson about his plans for the night and asks him to invite Jen; Jen is talking to Roger	23:59

21	Dawson invites Jen to the movies	25:05
22	boardwalk: Dawson tells Joey about his date with Jen and begs her to come along so that Jen will not feel awkward with two boys	25:35
23	Jen's house: she has another argument with her grandma about church, but is allowed to go to the movies, has to be back by ten o'clock	26:21
24	Dawson's house: Dawson and his dad watch his mom on TV, they talk about sex; Dawson leaves for his date	27:51
25	Joey's house: her sister shows her how to use lipstick; she leaves for the movies	29:02
26	sidewalk downtown: Dawson, Pacey, Joey and Jen are walking to the movie theatre; Jen tries to be nice to her, but Joey's reaction is very rude	29:56
27	inside the cinema: they take their seats; Pacey spots Tamara and goes to talk to her Dawson holds Jen's hand, Joey gets upset and makes embarrassing remarks, Dawson pulls her outside	30:47
28	Pacey sits next to Tamara; when her date comes with popcorn, they get into a fight and Pacey has to leave	32:19
29	lobby of the movie theatre: Dawson and Joey are very upset, she tells him that her behaviour is a result of his ignoring her since Jen arrived, then she leaves	33:12
30	Jen's yard: Dawson walks Jen home; they talk about the evening and almost kiss; Grams is watching them, Jen goes inside	33:59
31	docks downtown: Pacey meets Tamara, she claims that Pacey misunderstood her, telling him that she was not flirting with him; they end up in a kiss, but then she leaves, shocked at what has happened	35:47
32	Dawson's room: he finds Joey in his closet, they talk about what happened that night and agree on "growing up" as the reason for their problems; she leaves	37:31
33	dock at Dawson's house: when Joey starts rowing away in her boat she witnesses Dawson's mom kissing her co-anchor good night	41:34
credentials		41:52–42:24

Synopsis of Dawson's Creek: "Emotions in Motion" (pilot, first episode)

The episode analised in this unit is the very first episode of the series (the pilot) that was aired in the USA January 20, 1998. It is entitled *Emotions in Motion* and has a running time of 42 minutes. At the beginning the viewer learns that Dawson and Joey have been best friends since they were little kids. They even used to spend Saturday nights together in Dawson's bed. But they are 15 now and Joey tells him that since they are growing up she cannot sleep over any more. Dawson is able to persuade her that nothing has changed and she stays, not really convinced. When they meet Jen (a new girl from New York who has come to stay with her grandparents in Capeside) the following day Dawson feels attracted to her and this makes Joey feel jealous and behave in a an unfriendly way towards Jen.

After school Dawson and his buddy Pacey work at a video store where Pacey starts flirting with an older woman who turns out to be Tamara Jacobs, his new English teacher. When he learns that she is going to the movies that night, Pacey decides to go, too. Since he doesn't want it to look like he is following her, he asks Dawson to come along and suggests that he invites Jen. Since Dawson does not want Jen to feel uncomfortable with two boys he also asks Joey who finally agrees. Upset by Dawson timidly holding Jen's hand in the theatre Joey makes rude remarks to such an extent that Dawson gets furious and takes her to the lobby to talk. She accuses him of ignoring her since Jen's arrival and leaves. Dawson walks Jen home. They almost kiss before saying good night.

Pacey tries to sit next to Tamara in the theatre, but she prefers to be with her date. They meet later at the harbour and discuss their situation. Pacey insists on his assumption that Tamara flirted with him, Tamara tries to make him understand that she only rented a video. They end up in a kiss, but Tamara then leaves quickly, shocked at her own behaviour.

When Dawson gets home that night he finds a confused Joey in his closet. They talk things over, she tries to explain her behaviour to him and he reassures her that his feelings for her have not changed.

When Joey leaves Dawson's house, she sees Dawson's mom (a TV news anchor) kiss her co-anchor goodnight.

Unterrichtsempfehlungen

Als Einstieg in die Arbeit mit der Fernsehserie dient die Abbildung des DVD Covers (*Dawson's Creek: Season One*), auf dem die vier Hauptdarsteller sowie ein Kartenausschnitt der amerikanischen Nordostküste zur geographischen Orientierung zu sehen sind. Die Schüler sollten zunächst Gelegenheit erhalten, sich spontan dazu zu äußern. Es ist damit zu rechnen, dass einigen Schülern die Serie bekannt ist. Das kurze Zitat zum Inhalt der Serie (*"Four friends in a small coastal town help each other cope with adolescence"*) gibt mit dem Stichwort *adolescence* einen weiteren Hinweis auf mögliche Themen von *Dawson's Creek*, über die die Schüler in Form des *Alphabet of teenage life* spekulieren. Die Antworten können auf Folie oder einem Plakat festgehalten werden. Im Laufe der Unterrichtsreihe (oder an deren Ende) kann überprüft werden, welche Themen tatsächlich zur Sprache kommen.

Find more words for each letter of the alphabet that are related to a teenager's life.

Possible solution:

> A: adult, adventure, action, amazement, alcohol, attention, alone, angry
> B: boyfriend, body, burger, boys, beer, bands, buddy, believe
> C: clubs, chaos, curious, clothes, coke, chocolate, concert, change, couple, cell phone
> D: difficult, DJ, drinking, drugs, dance, DVD, drivers's license, dream
> E: energy, enjoy, eager, easiness, end, education, embarrassment
> F: fun, friends, film, future, first love, freedom, feelings, forget, fight
> G: girls, games, graduation, grow up, gym, gay
> H: homework, holiday, hurt, heart, hate, hobby, hip-hop, hangover
> I: independence, ignore, imagine, interest, ideal, intense, isolation
> J: jeans, jogging, job, jealousy, jaywalk, jeer, joke, justice
> K: kiss, kindness, keep together, key, knowledge, ketchup
> L: lonely, love, lifestyle, loser, literature, lies, lovesick
> M: music, movies, make-up, mobile phone, meaning, mess
> N: noisy, nosy, network, need, normal, notion, never
> O: opinion, object, obnoxious, obsession, offend, open-minded
> P: parents, party, peer-group, piercing, passionate, pair, present
> Q: qualification, question, quarrel, quest, quiet
> R: relationship, romance, run away, radio, radical, rap music
> S: stylish, sad, sleep, silly, surprise, strange, sex, stress, school
> T: TV, truth, time, tattoo, telephone, tough, touchy, tradition
> U: unhappy, ugly, understand, underwear, underground, unsure, underdog
> V: victim, video game, valentine, vague, values, virtue, vivacity
> W: wild, weekend, wish, wait, wage, want, wear, weird
> X: xerox, xenophobic, Xmas, XXL
> Y: young, yearn for, year, yuppie, yell
> Z: zealous, zest, zapping, zodiac

Eine kurze Internetrecherche zu Kevin Williamson als Schreiber von *Dawson's Creek* und Steven Spielberg als Lieblingsregisseur und beruflichem Vorbild von Hauptfigur Dawson Leery, auf den in der Folge mehrfach Bezug genommen wird, soll die *pre-viewing* Phase abschließen.

Dawson's Creek was created by Kevin Williamson. In the film, Dawson says that Steven Spielberg is his favourite director. Gather information on these people and be prepared to give a two-minute talk on them. You could go to www.imdb.com to get the information.

Possible solution

> **Kevin Williamson:** s. o.
> **Steven Spielberg:** born in 1946 in Cincinnati, Ohio, USA. One of the most successful, influencial and wealthiest filmmakers in the history of film. He is the producer and director of numerous critically acclaimed movies, including the following:
> Director-filmography: *War of the Worlds* 2005, *Catch Me If You Can* 2002, *Jurassic Park,*

1997, *Schindler's List* 1993, *Hook* 1991, *Indiana Jones And The Last Crusade* 1989, *The Color Purple* 1985, *E. T. the Extra-Terrestial* 1982, *Jaws* 1975.

Producer-filmography: *Munich* 2005, *Memoirs Of A Geisha* 2005, *Men In Black II* 2002, *Shrek* 2001, *Saving Private Ryan* 1998, *Amistad* 1997, *Schindler's List* 1993, *Arachnophobia* 1990, *Gremlins* 1984, *Poltergeist* 1982, *E. T.* 1982.

Allgemeine Unterrichtsempfehlungen zur Behandlung der Szenenfolgen

Die dem Schülerbuch *People Around You* zugrunde liegende Folge von Dawson's Creek ist in vier Teile (Parts I–IV) unterteilt, die sich auf die Haupthandlung (Entwicklung der Beziehung zwischen Dawson, Jen und Joey) und die Nebenhandlung (Beziehung zwischen Pacey und Tamara) beziehen. Die Zählwerkangaben im Szenenprotokoll (S. 132 f.) ermöglichen ein rasches Auffinden der Szenen mittels Nutzung des schnellen Vorlaufs mit doppelter oder vierfacher Geschwindigkeit.

Es empfiehlt sich, den Film nicht Szene für Szene vorzuführen und zu besprechen, sondern im Sinne eines ganzheitlich-analytischen Verfahrens in inhaltlichen Blöcken. Es ist also notwendig, dass die „hardware" (DVD-Player und Monitor) nicht nur für die einmalige Präsentation des ganzen Films, sondern wiederholt für die kontinuierliche Arbeit zur Verfügung stehen muss. Ersatzweise können jedoch gelegentlich Folien von Standbildern oder Audiomitschnitte von Dialogen eingesetzt werden. Zahlreiche Aufgaben im Schülerbuch werden ohnehin im Anschluss an die Besprechung im Plenum in Individual- bzw. Gruppenarbeit oder als Hausaufgabe bearbeitet, ohne dass die „hardware" zur Verfügung stehen muss.

Die Behandlung einer Szenenfolge sollte mehrere Schritte umfassen.
- Erste Präsentation zwecks Erfassung des Grobverständnisses
- Klärung von Verständnisschwierigkeiten
- Zweite Präsentation mit anschließenden Schüleräußerungen und Besprechungsvorschlägen
- Analyse der Szenenfolge im Plenum
- Diese soll grundsätzlich die folgenden drei Aspekte umfassen: a) What is (are) the scene(s) about? b) What cinematic devices does the director use to present the action? c) What is the function/message of the scene(s)?
- Nachbereitende (schriftliche) Aufgaben im Klassenraum oder in der Hausarbeit

Hinweise zur Verständnissicherung:

Es empfiehlt sich die Nutzung der chronologisch angelegten Vokabelzusammenstellung (Schülerbuch S. 131 ff.), die die Schüler/innen auch während der Videodarbietung einsehen können. Dennoch können insbesondere bei längeren Dialogpassagen (z. B. Gespräch zwischen Joey und Dawson: in der „pre-credit sequence", im Anschluss an den Kinobesuch oder am Ende des Films in Dawsons Studio) Verständnisschwierigkeiten auftreten.

Hier bieten sich mehrere Möglichkeiten zur Klärung an.
- Langsamer Rücklauf kürzerer Filmausschnitte und erneutes, ggf. mehrmaliges Vorspielen derselben und Besprechung im Plenum

- Gemeinsame Erarbeitung eines Dialogausschnitts anhand eines Standbildes (Betätigung der Standbildtaste), wobei das Ergebnis nur sinngemäß dem Original zu entsprechen braucht
- Einblendung der englischen Untertitel
- Einsatz des Filmscripts (Internet: www.angelfire.com/ks/descripts/100.html) als kompletter Text oder Lückentext

Der Unterricht soll entsprechend der Anlage des Schülerbuches und des auf ihn bezogenen Aufgabenapparats von einer lehrergesteuerten Bearbeitung des Films (Part I) ausgehen und allmählich zum selbstständigen Umgang mit dem audiovisuellen Medium (Part IV) führen. Bereits beim flüchtigen Durchblättern des Schülerbuches sowie des Lehrerkommentars fällt auf, dass der erste Teil des Films recht ausführlich behandelt wird und im Aufgabenapparat stark lehrer- und lehrbuchgesteuert ist. Und dies mit Bedacht: Die Schüler/innen werden kleinschrittig an Betrachtungsweisen und Analyseverfahren herangeführt, um in nachfolgenden Teilen selbstständiger im Sinne eines „student centred approach" mit dem Film umgehen zu können.

In die Inhaltsanalyse der einzelnen Filmteile sollte ein schrittweises Erschließen der wichtigsten filmischen Gestaltungsmittel eingebunden werden. In diesen Erschließungsprozess lassen sich kleine schüleraktivierende Projekte integrieren (siehe Schülerbuch S. 113, 114, 115 und 117). Die Schüler/innen erstellen ein Glossar mit ausgewählten Filmbegriffen, in dem die Erläuterungen durch entsprechende Bilder ergänzt werden. Karteikarten bieten den Vorteil, dass das Glossar beliebig erweitert werden kann und auch einzelne Karten leicht ausgetauscht werden können. Alternativ können die Definitionen auch auf den oberen Rand einzelner Blätter geschrieben werden. Darunter wird zur Illustration mindestens ein passendes Bild geklebt. Ideal wären Bilder aus Filmen mit kurzen Informationen zum Titel des Films, Genre, Name des Regisseurs, der Hauptdarsteller sowie des Erscheinungsjahres. Sowohl Karteikarten als auch Blätter sollten (in Klarsichthüllen) in einem Ordner abgeheftet werden.

Die Berufsbezeichnungen der an der Produktion eines Films beteiligten Personen und deren Definitionen (die im Schülerbuch auf Seite 109 herausgearbeitet wurden) können in das Glossar ebenfalls aufgenommen werden.

Pre-credit sequence and opening credits

Assignments – Solutions

Pre-credit sequence:

Write down all the information you get on Joey and Dawson.

- They like to watch movies and know a lot about cinema.
- They are fifteen years old.
- Joey has spent Saturday night with him since they were seven.
- They start high school the following Monday.
- Dawson's mom co-anchors for the local TV news.

- Joey thinks she is too old to sleep over any more.
- Dawson is convinced that their relationship will not change, even though they are getting older.

Describe their relationship and possible future problems.

> They have been best friends since they were little kids. They seem to be soulmates because they share an interest for movies, talk openly and feel very much at ease in each other's company.
> Since they are growing up a lot of things are changing for them and possible future problems can result from the fact that "the male/female thing will get in the way" and alter their relationship. This could mean that they fall in love with each other or one of them falls in love with another person.

Opening credits:

Watch the opening credits (03:15 – 04:20) and explain their function.

> The opening credits introduce the viewer to the characters and the setting. Moreover they present a list with the names of all the people that were involved in the making of the film.

Part I: Newcomers in town (pre-credit – scene 12)

Synopsis of the scenes

Part I introduces the setting and the main characters as well as the potential problems.
Within the main plot the viewer learns about the long and close friendship that exists between Joey and Dawson. So he will probably assume that this friendship will be endangered by the arrival of Jen.
Within the subplot, Dawson's friend Pacey meets the older and very attractive Tamara and trouble seems to be unavoidable.
Apart from these two storylines part I mentions a possible affair between Dawson's mum and her co-anchor and Jen's and her grandma's diverging attitudes towards religion.

Unterrichtsempfehlungen

Die Schüler/innen werden im ersten Teil des Films recht kleinschrittig an Seh- und Betrachtungsweisen sowie Analyseverfahren herangeführt (s. o. Allgemeine Empfehlungen).
Diesem Teil kommt insbesondere die Aufgabe zu, die Grundlage für die Entwicklung der Hand-

lung zu legen. Nachdem der Zuschauer in der *pre-credit sequence* mit zwei wichtigen Figuren (Joey und Dawson) bekannt gemacht worden ist, werden in den Szenen 2–7 die weiteren Protagonisten des Films eingeführt (Jen, Tamara und Pacey). Diese ca. dreizehn Minuten laufenden Szenen sollten daher unbedingt als Einheit vorgeführt und besprochen werden.

In eine Tabelle an der Tafel, die nach und nach ergänzt werden kann, könnten im Verlauf des Unterrichtsgesprächs alle Informationen eingetragen werden, die der Film vermittelt.

	What they look like	How they behave
Dawson		
Joey		
Jen		
Tamara		
Pacey		

Die Szenen 8–12 mit einer Laufzeit von ca. 6 Minuten schließen sich an, so dass sich bereits hier eine Ergänzung der obigen Tabelle anbietet.

Filmsprachlich sind „field size" (Schülerbuch S. 113) und „point of view" mithilfe von Standbildern (Schülerbuch S. 114) einzuführen und von den Schülern in Miniprojekten zu verarbeiten.

Anmerkung: Die Musik, die die Szene zu Beginn unterstützt, ist das Lied *As I Lay me Down* (Album: Whaler) von Sophie B. Hawkins mit folgendem Text:
"It felt like spring time on this February morning
In the courtyard birds were singing your praise
I'm still recalling things you said to make me feel alright
I carried them with me today now.
… "

Assignments – Solutions

Scene 2: The new girl in town

1. Watch scene two without sound and explain what happens.

> While Joey is glaring angrily at Pacey a taxi arrives and a beautiful girl steps out. The teenagers introduce themselves. Whereas the boys are delighted to meet the new girl, Joey makes a face.

2. Watch the scene again with sound and add missing information.

> We hear that the girl's name is Jen. She has come from New York to help her grandmother with her sick grandfather. They are Dawson's neighbours and she lets him know that they have met before. They find out that they will all go to the same school, tenth grade.

3. Describe the cinematic devices the director employs to show that Jen is an attractive girl and that her appearance impresses Dawson and Pacey.

- soft, bright colors
- soft sunlight
- slow motion
- She wears a short dress.
- The wind is playing with her hair and her dress.
- The boys hurry to meet her.
- soft music
- lyrics: "Hey pretty girl"
- The enchanted expressions on the boys' faces.
- Pacey says: "Well, my mouth drops."
- Joey seems to be jealous (facial expression).
- Jen is mostly positioned in the middle of the screen.

4. How do we know that Joey is not so happy to meet Jen?

Joey's facial expressions reveal that she is really disgusted by Jen's arrival. She obviously fakes a smile, lets it fade quickly to remain sullen, watching Jen leave with a very angry expression on her face. It is thus the subtext in this scene that lets the viewer know that Joey is not happy to meet Jen.

5. The scene ends with a close-up of Dawson's smiling face watching Jen leave (06:28). Put yourself in Dawson's position and write a one-line voice-over text for him that reveals his feelings at this moment.

- Wow!
- She's so beautiful.
- I hope I'll see her sooner than Monday.
- What a challenge!
- Jesus, she's pretty.
- Does she have a boyfriend?
- …

6. What function does the scene have and what future events might the film be hinting at?

The function of the scene is to show that something in the friends' relationship has changed with Jen's arrival. The boys openly demonstrate their admiration and male interest in the new girl, provoking Joey's disapproval and female jealousy. She clearly sees a rival in Jen. The close-up of Dawson's smiling face at the end of the scene suggests that he will fall in love with Jen. The technical term for this hinting at events to come is *foreshadowing*.

Part I: Newcomers in town (pre-credit – scene 12)

Scenes 5–7: "The new lady in town"

1. Describe Pacey's experience with Tamara Jacobs.

> When Pacey is working with Dawson at the local video store after school he is struck by the beauty of an older woman who is new in town and wants to rent a video. She is quite aware of the impression she is making on Pacey and asks for the video of *The Graduate*. She explains that that is the movie where an older woman seduces a young man, clearly alluding to Pacey and herself. When she leaves Pacey is convinced that she was flirting with him.

2. How does the film show that Pacey and Tamara like each other?

> The following cinematic devices show that Pacey and Tamara like each other:
> - Pacey stands up straight when he notices Tamara entering the store.
> - He breathes in and stares at her while she is approaching him.
> - Tamara focuses on Pacey (not on Dawson).
> - They often look and smile at each other.
> - They introduce each other and shake hands.
> - When she tells him that she is in the mood for romance he stammers a little.
> - Dawson is aware that something is going on between Pacey and Tamara. He looks at them, smiling.
> - When they talk about *The Graduate* Pacey breathes heavily.
> - When Tamara leaves, she turns around and looks straight into Pacey's eyes.

3. What does the encounter with Tamara mean for Pacey?

> The encounter with Tamara raises Pacey's hopes that he can have an affair with an older, experienced woman. He is sure that she must feel attracted to him because he is a virile young man.

4. Re-tell the incident from Dawson's point-of-view.

> "When I was working at the video store with Pacey the door opened and a woman we didn't know came in. I must admit she was extremely attractive – for her age. Poor Pacey really fell for her. He was so impressed he couldn't even think straight. You could actually feel the tension between them in the air. The moment she asked for *The Graduate* I knew that she was teasing my buddy, but he was sure she was seriously flirting with him. How embarrassing! Now he's dreaming of having an affair with her. He hasn't got the slightest chance. That woman is far too beautiful and experienced for him."

5. Look up the different points-of-view for the camera in the glossary and find the appropriate term for each of the following stills from scenes 5–7.

> Solution (pictures from left to right):
> 1) establishing shot   3) point-of-view shot
> 2) over-the-shoulder shot   4) reverse-angle shot

6. Watch scenes 5–7 again and identify different points-of-view. What effect do the changing points-of-view have on the viewer?

> The establishing shot of the video store from the outside at the beginning gives the viewer an idea of the location of the scene that follows. The frequently changing points-of-view that the camera assumes make the dialogue in these scenes lively. When we are in the store, the camera first shows Pacey and Dawson in a point-of-view shot. The viewer can easily imagine entering the store and seeing the two boys behind the counter.
> During the conversations in these scenes (between the boys and Nellie and between the boys, especially Pacey, and Tamara) the camera alternates betweeen point-of-view shots and reverse-angle shots of the characters involved. So the spectator gets views of both sides of the dialogue. He not only sees (and hears) what one person says, but also witnesses the other person's reaction.
> On various occasions the camera is positioned behind Nellie or Tamara and shows the boys and (part of) her shoulder (over-the-shoulder shot) so that the viewer can put himself easily in her position and experiences the moment from her point of view.

Scenes 8–12: "Dawson and the two girls"

1. When Dawson gets home after working at the video store he sees the following scene. Point out by what means the director achieves this romantic atmosphere.

> The following cinematic means contribute to the creation of this romantic scene:
> - soft, warm colours
> - beautiful landscape
> - gorgeous sunset
> - soft sunlight reflected in the still water of the creek
> - lonely girl sitting on the dock

2. How would you intensify this romantic effect?

> The romantic atmosphere could be intensified by romantic music.

3. Why does Dawson want to show his "studio" to Jen and how does she react?

> At the dock Dawson and Jen talk about Dawson's ambition to become a director and his admiration for Steven Spielberg. He wants to show her his room (which is full of film-related items such as movie posters, a framed picture of Stephen Spielberg and an E. T. doll) to make her understand his enthusiasm. She is impressed, but doesn't get too involved and teases him a little in a friendly, ironic way.

4. Describe Joey's feelings when she notices Jen in Dawson's room in one sentence.

> When Joey wants to enter Dawson's room (as usual through the window) and hears Jen talking to him, she feels disturbed, confused, upset.

5. Dawson talks with Jen and later with Joey. Do you think the encounter with the two girls will have any consequences?

> The film suggests that Dawson is really interested in Jen, but he does not see this as interfering with his relationship with Joey. He behaves like the close friend he has always been. Joey, on the other hand, feels irritated by Jen's appearance on the scene. She seems to be anticipating that Dawson will fall in love with Jen and that things will change for them.

6. What else did you see and hear in the first part of Dawson's Creek?

> Probable points:
> - Dawson's parents have a very close relationship. They are not embarrassed when Dawson and Pacey find them kissing in the living room.
> - Joey lives down the creek with her pregnant sister and black boyfriend. He is a cook.
> - Joey has a little argument with her sister about tidying up her room.
> - Nellie's father owns the video store.
> - Dawson thinks that his mom might be having an affair with her co-anchor.
> - Jen's granddad is lying unconscious in bed.
> - Jen has problems with her grandma because she is very religious and Jen confesses to being an atheist.
> - Jen's grandma tells her to stay away from Dawson and Joey because they spend the night together and do not go to church.
> - ...

Part II: First day at Capeside High (scenes 13–22)

Synopsis of the scenes

Part II provides a closer look at the characters. The problems that the viewer has already anticipated will develop. It becomes obvious that Joey feels annoyed by Jen's presence. Even though she assures her that she and Dawson are not a couple, she reacts in a hostile way to Jen's friendly approach and resents her obvious attraction to Dawson.
The fact that Pacey learns that Tamara is his new English teacher does not discourage him from arranging a "chance" encounter with her at the movies. He asks Dawson to invite Jen. Dawson agrees, but also begs Joey to join them.

Unterrichtsempfehlungen

Der ca. 9 Minuten dauernde zweite Teil, in dem die Handlung, aber auch die sog. Nebenhandlung weitergeführt wird, kann als Einheit präsentiert und behandelt werden.

Die Informationen, die der Film liefert, können im Unterrichtsgespräch in zwei „spidergrams" gesammelt werden.
Die Bearbeitung des recht umfangreichen Aufgabenapparats kann als Hausaufgabe oder teilweise in Kleingruppenarbeit in der Klasse erledigt werden.

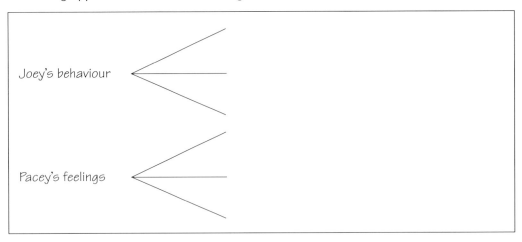

Die filmsprachlichen Mittel *camera angles* und *camera movement* werden in der bekannten Weise eingeführt und durch Miniprojekte vertieft.
Teil II ist auch der Ort der Einführung filmischer Schnitttechniken, die zeigen, wie ein Film von einem Bild ins nächste übergeht (*punctuation*), sowie des Hinweises auf Möglichkeiten, die dem Cutter am Schneidebrett zur Verfügung stehen, um einzelne Bilder oder Szenen miteinander in Beziehung zu setzen (*editing, montage*). Die Schüler/innen sollen erfahren, dass Szenen nicht zusammenhängend ohne Unterbrechung aufgenommen werden. Einzelne Einstellungen werden in der Phase der Produktion mehrmals gedreht, oft mit großem zeitlichen Abstand. Danach wählt der *Cutter* (*editor*) in der Phase der *post production* die jeweils besten Aufnahmen aus, schneidet sie und setzt sie oft in veränderter Reihenfolge neu zu einer kohärenten Einheit zusammen.
Eine Möglichkeit, dieses Vorgehen zu veranschaulichen, ist die Vorführung von Filmfehlern (*filmmistakes, goofs*). Die häufigsten Filmfehler sind Anschlussfehler (*continuity mistakes*), die bei den o.g. Verfahren entstehen. Der aufmerksame Zuschauer kann anhand dieser Fehler erkennen, dass der Film geschnitten wurde. Als Beispiel mag eine Szene aus dem Film *Clueless* dienen, zu dem auf Seite 121 des Schülerbuches eine Rezension abgedruckt ist:
„Während ihrer Führerscheinprüfung beschädigt die Protagonistin Cher den Autospiegel, der jedoch beim folgenden Abbiegen unbeschädigt ist."
Falls diese DVD nicht zur Verfügung steht, sei für weitere Beispiele auf die Internetseite www.moviemistakes.com verwiesen, auf der zu sehr vielen Filmen Filmfehler beschrieben werden.
Selbstverständlich können auch die Schüler aufgefordert werden, Beispiele zu sammeln und in der Klasse vorzustellen.
Das *Mini project* „Punctuation and editing" mit der Aufgabe, Beispiele für verschiedene Montage- und Schnitttechniken auf DVDs zu finden, dient einerseits dazu, einen Film zielgerichtet anzusehen. Andererseits werden auf diese Weise die abstrakten Begriffe durch konkrete Filmbilder ergänzt und so nachvollziehbarer und einprägsamer.
Als Alternative bietet sich ein Besuch der Webseite www.filmsite.org/filmterms an, die Erläuterungen der Filmbegriffe und Beispielszenen aus bekannten Filmen bietet.

Assignments – Solutions

1. Describe Joey's reaction to meeting Jen in her biology class. Can you think of any reasons why she does not like Jen?

> When Jen is sitting in her biology room, waiting for the class to start, Jen comes in, looking around. Joey rolls her eyes and tries to hide, raising her hand to her face and looking the other way. But Jen spots her and sits down next to her. When Jen tries to start a friendly conversation, Joey does not respond. She keeps her distance, remaining coolly polite.

2. Why does the film show Pacey balancing a book on his head before the teacher enters the room?

> The scene shows Pacey balancing a book on his head to remind the viewer that he is a normal 10th grader (not an adult). His behaviour could even be described as a little childish.

3. How does Tamara react when she sees Pacey as a student in her class?

> When Tamara comes into the classroom and realises that Pacey is one of her new students she reacts in a very professional, adult way. She does not show any surprise, embarrassment or any other emotion.

4. How is the idea of an exciting first day at school conveyed by means of cinematic devices?

> - We hear loud, fast music.
> - We see lots of activities: students are talking, throwing frisbees, skateboarding, etc.
> - The scene is full of movement: the camera and the students move.
> - zoom-in, zoom-out

5. How does the cameraman emphasise Pacey's feelings when he learns that Tamara is his new English teacher?

> When Pacey realises that Tamara is his new English teacher the camera zooms in on him and ends in a close-up of his face, thus revealing his emotions by focusing on his facial expression.

6. Write a short voice-over text for him that reveals his feelings and thoughts at this moment.

> Possible solution:
> Oh – my – God! Does this mean I'm lucky? No, forget it, she's my teacher, and teachers are … . But hey, she was flirting with me in the video store. I'm sure she fancied me. I can feel it. Yes, Miss Jacobs, we'll get together. I just have to figure out the right strategy …

7. How does the cameraman stress that Pacey feels quite self-confident when he talks to Tamara in the teachers' room?

> When Pacey talks to Tamara in the teachers' room he is standing in front of her. She is sitting at a table, looking up at him. The camera is positioned behind Tamara, filming Pacey from her point-of-view. So Pacey is shown from a low angle and that makes him appear self-confident. He appears taller/larger and is looking down at her.

8. Why does Pacey ask Dawson to invite Jen to the movies?

> Since Pacey knows that Tamara will be at the movies that night, he thinks it is his chance to meet her privately. But he cannot ask her for a date. He wants the meeting to look accidental and does not want to go alone. So when he is at the theatre with his friends he can pretend to meet Tamara by accident. Apart from that he thinks he is doing Dawson a favour when he urges him to invite Jen because he knows that Dawson really likes Jen.

9. Comment on the 'double date'.

> Die Kommentare werden natürlich sehr unterschiedlich ausfallen, sollen sie doch die persönliche Meinung eines jeden einzelnen Schülers zu der Idee ausdrücken, das Dawson neben Jen auch noch Joey ins Kino einlud, damit Jen sich allein mit zwei Jungen nicht unwohl fühlt.

10. While watching scenes 21–23 pay special attention to the way the individual scenes are linked and identify the punctuation devices used by the editor.

> At the end of scene 21 there is a match cut from the hall of the school where Dawson invites Jen to the movies to the boardwalk where Joey is walking home. The scenes are linked by aural parallelism because the romantic instrumental music of scene 21 continues into scene 22. At the end of scene 22 we see a fade-out, followed by a fade-in to scene 23 at Jen's house.

11. What else did you see and hear in scenes 13–22?

> - Dawson is very disappointed because he is not allowed to join the film class.
> - Jen asks Joey whether she and Dawson are a pair, but she tells her that they are just friends.
> - Joey's mother died of cancer.
> - Joey's father is in jail because of a drug-related problem.
> - Joey asks Jen not to abuse Dawson's feelings.
> - …

Part III: A night at the movies (scenes 23–29)

Synopsis of the scenes

Part III clearly reveals Joey's jealousy. When she notices Dawson holding Jen's hand, she makes some really rude remarks about Jen. So Dawson drags her out to the lobby of the movie theater where she loses her temper and accuses him of ignoring her since Jen's arrival. The presence of Tamara's companion does not stop Pacey from flirting with her and he ends up in a fight.

Unterrichtsempfehlungen

Da den Schülern im Laufe der Unterrichtsreihe Verfahren der Filmanalyse vermittelt worden sind, können sie ihr erworbenes Wissen nun bei der Untersuchung dieses Teils der Episode selbstständig anwenden. Da eine Vielzahl und Vielfalt von Informationen übermittelt wird, bietet sich eine arbeitsteilige Gruppenarbeit an, bei der sich jede Gruppe auf zwei filmtechnische Aspekte konzentriert. Der Inhalt (*action, dialogue*) wird allerdings von allen Gruppen kurz wiedergegeben. Zur Vorbereitung übertragen die Schüler den im Schülerbuch auf S. 118 abgedruckten Beobachtungsbogen in ihre Hefte und legen ihn für die drei zu untersuchenden Szenen dreispaltig an.
Nach der Gruppeneinteilung und Klärung der Arbeitsaufträge werden die betreffenden Szenen mindestens zweimal (mit kurzen Unterbrechungen zur Anfertigung von Notizen) vorgespielt. Nach der Erledigung des Arbeitsauftrags werten die Gruppenmitglieder ihre Ergebnisse innerhalb ihrer Gruppe aus, einigen sich auf einen Text und schließlich auf einen Sprecher, der die Ergebnisse im Plenum präsentiert. Bei der Präsentation sollte der DVD-Spieler zur Verfügung stehen und eingesetzt werden.
Der Beobachtungsbogen kann allgemein als Beispiel für die Analyse von Filmszenen dienen. Die Schüler/innen sollten jedoch darauf aufmerksam gemacht werden, dass nicht immer unbedingt jede Spalte/Zeile ausgefüllt werden muss. Dies macht nur dann Sinn, wenn das beobachtete Phänomen die inhaltliche Aussage unterstützt. Die Aufgaben ermöglichen ein Wiedererkennen der zuvor erarbeiteten Gesichtspunkte der Filmanalyse und schulen die Beobachtungsgabe der Schüler. Die Rubrik „your comment" dient zum Eintrag filmtechnischer Aspekte, die für besonders erwähnenswert gehalten werden.
Die Musik, die am Ende von Szene 25 (Bessie zeigt ihrer Schwester Joey, wie man einen Lippenstift benutzt) und am Anfang von Szene 26 (die vier Jugendlichen auf dem Weg zum Kino) im Hintergrund ertönt, ist das Lied *Good Mother* von Jann Arden. (Album: Living Under June). Der Text unterstützt und kommentiert die Handlung, den Dialog und die Bilder und kann zur Analyse mit herangezogen werden.
Da die Worte nicht so leicht zu verstehen sind, könnte der kurze Text an die Tafel geschrieben werden.

„I've never wanted anything
No I've, no I've, I've never
Wanted anything
So bad ... so bad."

Die Musik ist aber auch ohne den Text deutlich als freundlich und romantisch zu erkennen; sie bricht abrupt in dem Moment ab, in dem Joey sehr unhöflich auf eine freundliche Frage von Jen reagiert. Jen: "Hey Joey, I love your lipstick. What shade is that?" Joey: "Wicked Red. Uh, I love your hair color, what number is that?"

Assignments – Solutions

While watching scenes 26–28 fill in the following viewing grid. Split into four groups. Everybody makes notes on action and dialogue. Additional tasks for each group:
Group 1: Concentrates on field size and point of view.
Group 2: Concentrates on camera movement and camera angle.
Group 3: Concentrates on punctuation and editing.
Group 4: Concentrates on light(ing), music and sound.

scene	26	27	28
action	downtown: Pacey, Dawson, Joey and Jen are walking to the movie theatre. Jen tries to start a friendly conversation but Joey is really rude.	inside the theatre: the four teens take their seats. When Pacey spots Tamara, he goes to talk to her. Dawson holds Jen's hand, Joey makes rude remarks; Dawson drags her outside.	Pacey sits down next to Tamara and starts a conversation. Then her date comes with popcorn. They argue, the popcorn is spilled on the person behind them and he punches Pacey in the face.
dialogue	Joey: "I love your hair color. What number is it? – Are you a virgin? Dawson: "You've got to excuse Joey. – What's up with you?"	Joey: "How important is size to you?" Dawson: "You and me. Outside. Now."	Tamara: "Look Pacey, you have to understand, I was only renting a movie."
field size	mostly medium long shots and medium shots	close-ups of faces as they watch the movie	close-ups of faces
point-of-view	establishing shot	establishing shot p-o-v-shot: Joey watching the hands	over-the shoulder p-o-v reverse angle
camera angle	straight-on angle; end: overhead shot	straight-on angle low angle on Pacey	straight-on angle high angle on Pacey; low angle on Benji

camera movement	tracking shot zoom-out	zoom-in on Dawson, Jen and Joey when the lights dim pan to Dawson's hand	pan over to Pacey sitting next to Tamara
punctuation	scene 25/26: cut scene 26/27: cut to the inside of the movie theatre	scene 26/27: cut to the inside of the theatre; scene 27/28: cut to Tamara	27/28: cut to Tamara 28/29: cut to the lobby of the movie theatre
editing	match cut (music of previous scene continues)		
light, colours	twilight; lights in store windows; the teenagers wear light, soft-coloured summer clothes	lights dim when the movie begins; dark (low key) lighting	dim lights
sound	romantic music in the background later: instrumental, easy-listening music	quiet instrumental, expectant music in the background; when Dawson tries to hold Jen's hand: more dramatic music, like in a cartoon or comedy	at the beginning: a person in the movie talking no music
your comment	The romantic music stops the moment Joey gives a very rude answer to Jen's friendly question.	The pan to the close-up of Dawson's and Jen's hands from Joey's point-of-view, supported by dramatic music clearly stresses what Joey is getting so upset about.	When Tamara tells Pacey that she was not flirting with him, the camera emphasises his confusion and doubts by showing a close-up of his face.

Scene 29: "I thought you were my friend"

Die folgende Aufgabe fordert auf, die schauspielerische Leistung und die Kameraführung genau zu beobachten und zu beschreiben. Auf diese Weise sollen die Schüler nachvollziehen, wie die explosive Atmosphäre dieser Szene geschaffen wird.

150 Reel or real? – A television series

1. Watch scene 29 closely and add the instructions for the actors and camerateam that a scriptwriter would add to the transcript of the dialogue in your exercise books. Think of gestures, mime, tone of voice, movements, field sizes, camera angles, etc.

1. No music. Close-up of their faces. Point-of-view shot. Straight-on angle. They are standing very close, looking at each other. Dawson shouts angrily at her, raising his voice furiously. He is outraged.
2. Joey shouts back at him in an aggressive, high tone of voice, pronouncing every single word clearly. She brings her face closer to his while shouting.
3. Dawson briefly looks away, closing his eyes, unnerved.
4. Still looking intently at each other. Joey's voice is very intense. Her eyes move rapidly while looking into his eyes.
5. Still shouting. He looks at her desperately.
6. She snarls at him. Her face is resolute.
7. Joey turns away, shaking her head, walking off. He stares after her, unsure how to respond, then calls her in a calm, but determined way.
8. She turns around, looks at him openly. Over-the-shoulder shot. Dawson's point-of-view.'
Joey sounds still upset.
9. Close-up of Dawson's startled face. He looks at her squarely. Calmly.
10. Close-up of Joey's face. She moves close to him. Over-the-shoulder shot (her point-of-view); reverse-angle shot, over-the shoulder-shot (his point-of-view).
11. Joey leaves, first backwards, shaking her head. Then she turns, not looking back. Close-up of Dawson's upset face. Fade-out (to black).

2. In groups of three, discuss Joey's behaviour in scene 29. Present your results to the class.

Students will probably agree on the idea that Joey is jealous.

3. In small groups or pairs, translate the dialogue into German. Read it out while playing the scene again without sound. Then compare with German subtitles on the DVD (or the dubbed German version).

Bei der Übersetzung geht es natürlich nicht um eine wortgetreue Übertragung ins Deutsche, sondern darum, die Situation und Stimmung möglichst adäquat wieder zu geben. Die Übersetzungen der Schüler werden sehr unterschiedlich ausfallen, wobei die wenigsten wohl als „falsch" bezeichnet werden können. Der Vergleich mit der auf der DVD angebotenen Version macht dies auch deutlich, wird er doch noch weitere Versionen liefern und zur Diskussion herausfordern.
Die Stelle, an der Dawson *"Sue me"* sagt, kann zum Anlass genommen werden, kurz über kulturbedingte Probleme bei Übersetzungen zu sprechen. In den USA werden viele Prozesse um „Verbrechen" geführt (und gewonnen), die Europäern eher lächerlich und aussichtslos erscheinen und in Europa nicht vor Gericht kämen.

DAWSON: Bist du bescheuert? Was ist dein Problem?
JOEY: Mein Problem ist, dass du kein Wort mehr mit mir gesprochen hast, seitdem die kleine Miss Highlights hier aufgetaucht ist.

DAWSON: Blödsinn! Das ist reiner Blödsinn. Und das weißt du.
JOEY: Alles, was ich weiß, ist, dass deine Hormone verrückt spielen und dass du kein anderes menschliches Wesen mehr bemerkst.
DAWSON: Ich mag sie, okay? Verklag mich doch. Ich dachte, du wärst meine Freundin. Wo bleibt ein wenig Verständnis?
JOEY: Ich verstehe alles. Ich bin es leid. Ich tue nichts anderes als verstehen.
DAWSON: Joey!
JOEY: An dir geht alles vorbei, Dawson. Du bist so weit von der Realität entfernt, dass du noch nicht einmal siehst, was genau vor dir ist.
DAWSON: Wovon sprichst du?
JOEY: Von deinem Leben. Es ist ein verdammtes Märchen und du weißt es noch nicht mal. Du suchst nur nach Konflikten für das Skript, das du gerade schreibst. Hör auf, im Film zu leben. Werd erwachsen.

Part IV: The end of a night at the movies (scenes 30–33)

Synopsis of the scenes

Part IV shows how that night ends for the five characters. Dawson takes Jen home and apologises for the awful evening. They talk about their feelings for each other and would have kissed if Jen's grandma had not appeared at the door.
Pacey meets Tamara on the boardwalk. She tries to convince him that she was not flirting with him, but they end up kissing.
When Dawson gets home, he finds a confused Joey in his closet. They talk openly about their problems and agree that they are growing up and that their relationship is changing. When Joey runs to her boat she is crying. Dawson stays in his room, very upset and sad. But at the end he shouts something that calms her down and makes her laugh.

Unterrichtsempfehlungen

Die letzten Szenen der Folge sollen von den Schülern selbstständig unter Verwendung des *viewing grid* (Schülerbuch S. 125) untersucht werden. Auch für diesen Beobachtungsbogen gilt, dass nicht jedes Detail des Films aufgenommen zu werden braucht. Es kommt vielmehr darauf an, die für die Szene aussagekräftigsten Aspekte herauszugreifen und zu deuten.
Die Musik (I'll stand by you), die am Ende von Szene 32, als Joey traurig mit ihrem Ruderboot abfährt, erklingt und in dem Moment abbricht, als Joey Dawsons Mutter sieht, stammt von den Pretenders (Album: Last Of The Independents).

Der Text lautet:

"Oh, why do you look so sad?
Tears are in your eyes
Come on and come to me
Don't be ashamed to cry.
Let me see you through
'cause I've seen the dark side too
When the night falls on you
You don't know what to do
Nothing you confess
Could make me love you less."

Assignments – Solutions

Analyse part IV of *Dawson's Creek* in pairs, using the viewing grid (p. 125). Get together in small groups and discuss your findings. Then present your results in class, using the DVD to illustrate your conclusions.

Part IV: The end of a night at the movies (scenes 30–33)

scene/ sequence	action, dialogue	cinematic devices	function, effects	function of the scene	theme, message	comment
30	Dawson walks Jen home. They almost kiss. Jen: "You are very sweet. Smart …."	romantic lighting, romantic music; close-ups	emphasise the feeling of falling in love	it reveals that Jen also likes Dawson.	A first date can have awkward moments.	a very romantic scene, spoiled at the end by Jen's grandma
31	Pacey meets Tamara at the docks. They kiss. Tamara: "You're wrong about one thing Pacey. You're not a boy."	changing points-of-view low angle on Pacey	discussion between two people Pacey feels self-confident	It shows that Pacey is very determined and that Tamara does feel attracted to him.	Even adults (including teachers) can lose control of a situation.	sarcastic comment by Pacey at the end of the scene. "I'll see you in school, Miss Jacobs."
32	Dawson finds Joey in his closet. They talk things over. She leaves. Dawson: "It's all so complicated." Joey: "We're growing up, Dawson, that's all."	high angle on Joey, sad music, sudden silence, lyrics. "I'll stand by you" cross-cutting	she feels confused end of childhood? decisive moment friends forever we see both sides	It shows that their relationship is strong.	Growing up is not easy. You should talk about your problems.	"repetition" of the pre-credit scene, but this time she does not spend the night
33	As she leaves, Joey witnesses Dawson's mom kissing her co-anchor good night.	dim lightning, close up of Joey's face fade-out (to dark)	secret? she is shocked what will happen next?	We discover that the marriage of Dawson's parents is not very stable/happy.	Things are not always what they seem.	Joey looks up at D.'s window to check if he has also seen the scene. She does not want him to suffer

Evaluating the film

1. Give a short outline of the main plot and the sub plot of the first episode.

Main plot: Joey and Dawson have been best friends since they were seven. She has been sleeping over at Dawson's every Saturday night. They are fifteen now and she feels that things are changing and that she should not sleep in his bed any more. He does not share her worries and insists on the assumption that nothing will alter their relationship.
When Jen, his neighbours' granddaughter arrives in town, he starts falling in love with her and Joey starts acting strange because she is jealous. At the end they have to acknowledge that things do change when you grow up.
Subplot: While working at the videostore Dawson's buddy Pacey starts flirting with an attractive older woman who turns out to be his new teacher, Miss Jacobs. When she mentions that she is going to the movies, he decides to go, too. He makes it look like he went with his friends and tries to sit next to Tamara in the theatre. But she prefers to be with her date and tells him that she was not flirting with him. When they meet again later that night Pacey accuses her of feeling attracted to him and they kiss.

2. What is the main theme of this episode? Do you see any connection between the beginning and the end?

The main theme of the first episode of *Dawson's Creek* could be "Falling in love for the first time."
The episode starts with the scene in Dawson's room when Joey tells him that she thinks they have grown up and she cannot sleep over any more. Dawson disagrees and persuades her to stay. At the end of the episode (scene 33) we almost see the same scene again. Again they talk about their changing relationship in Dawson's room at night. But this time they agree not to spend the night together any more and Joey leaves.

3. Write a character profile for one of the characters. It should explain the character's role in the film and give information on his or her biography and personality.

Dawson Leery, the central character and namesake of the series is an attractive 15 year old teenager. Blond hair, blue eyes, clear skin, slim, fit-looking. He wears casual, loose-fitting clothes.
His life seems perfect. He lives with his loving parents (his mother co-anchors the local TV news) in a comfortable home in the quiet, small seaside village of Capeside, MA.
Dawson is a sophomore at Capeside High School and works part-time at the local video store. He's a film buff and dreams of becoming a director. He has close friends: his buddy Pacey and best friend Joey.
Dawson is an idealistic, smart, romantic, passionate and sensitive boy.

4. In pairs, write a text for Dawson's Creek, episode I which could appear in a TV guide.

> Als Beispiel sei hier der Text des TV Guides (http://online.tvguide.com) abgedruckt:
> "Pilot Episode: Debut: A coming-of-age drama about four teens in a Boston suburb. In the opener, Dawson (James Van Der Beek) irks his best friend with his attraction to a neighbour, while pal Pacey (Joshua Jackson) fixates on their new teacher. Jen: Michelle Williams. Tamara: Leann Hunley. Mitch Leery: John Wesley Shipp."

Beyond the film

In small groups, write a script (including cinematic devices) for a possible following scene.

> Some ideas:
> - Monday at school: Joey feels ashamed of her behaviour at the movie theatre and apologises to Jen. They have a serious talk and start to become friends.
> - That night at Jen's house: Her grandma is furious about her starting a relationship with Dawson and threatens to send her back to New York.
> - The next morning at the lonely dock: Jen is sitting at the place where Dawson asked her if she wanted to see his studio. She is thinking of Dawson, hoping for him to come.
> - The following night at Jen's house: Dawson wants to see Jen, but her grandma wants to talk to him first. He has a hard time, but is finally able to convince her that he is not unsuitable and/or the wrong kind of boy for her granddaughter.

Appreciating a film: Reviews

What is the intention of a film critic who writes a review of a film?

> Basically, the intention of a film critic is to evaluate the film by pointing out its strengths and weaknesses so that the reader can make up his mind about going to see it. She will also be trying to impress the reader with his/her knowledge/taste/style, etc.

Where can you find reviews of films or TV programmes?

> You can find film reviews in the newspaper, in movie magazines, in TV guides, in the internet, on the radio.

Review of Clueless
by Gabriela Toth

Assignments – Solutions

1. Reveal the structure of the review of *Clueless* by subdividing it according to the topic covered and find a heading for each topic.

ll. 1–9: introduction
    (ll. 10–12: genre; ll. 12–14: theme)
ll. 15–22: plot outline
ll. 23–42: evaluation (strengths and weaknesses)
    ll. 26–30: dialogue
    ll. 31–42: characters
ll. 43–47: conclusion (recommendation)

2. Point out the parts where the critic clearly voices her personal opinion.

ll. 5–9/ll. 21 f./ll. 23–32/ll. 43–47

3. Write down some questions that the critic does not answer in her review.

- What is the message of the movie?
- How does it relate to other films?
- What was the performance of the actors like?
- How well did the actors perform their roles?
- …

4. Make a list of all the aspects that should be included in a good review.

– theme	– performance
– message	– camera work
– plot	– costume
– dialogue	– special effects
– characters	– verdict recommendation

5. Use these aspects as headings for a list of useful vocabulary for film reviews and start filling it in by finding appropiate words and expressions in the review of *Clueless*.
Add words and expresssions that you know or have looked up in a dictionary and add to the list whenever you read or write a review in the future.

Useful vocabulary for film reviews

general	**positive**: awesome, brilliant, enjoyable, has something for everybody, terrific, excellent, extraordinary, entertaining, inspiring, gripping, box-office success, blockbuster, a top-grossing film, … **negative**: disturbing, boring, a complete waste of time, box-office flop failure, …
characters	**positive**: interesting, you can learn something from, easy to relate to, original, complex, convincing, realistic, unforgettable … **negative**: unconvincing, unrealistic, weird, mindless, unappealing, boring, …
dialogue	**positive**: witty, snappy, quotable, colloquialisms, catch phrases, well-written, exceptional, humorous, memorable, meaningful, funny, heart-warming, smart, … **negative**: boring, long-winded, offensive, just not funny, dull, meaningless, useless, …
costume	**positive**: great, fascinating, wonderful, skilful, original, faultless, fine, stylish, … **negative**: tasteless, unpleasant, not authentic, …
plot	**positive**: plausible, realistic, interesting, surprising, unexpected, fast-paced, gripping, amusing, thrilling, delightful, … **negative**: confusing, questionable, improbable, predictable, sinister, inconsistent, …
camera operations	**positive**: unusual, eye-catching, stunning, flawless, overwhelming, sensational, impressive, professional, outstanding, … **negative**: weak, unimpressive, amateurish, …
special effects	**positive**: fast-paced, fantastic, marvellous, extraordinary, fascinating, spectacular, breathtaking, skilled, exciting, masterly, … **negative**: mediocre, disappointing, miserable, flawed, lousy, unconvincing, …
theme, message	**positive**: heartbreaking, involving, moving, encouraging, important, touching, … **negative**: far-fetched, superficial, shallow, shocking, questionable, poor, obvious, strange, …
performance	**positive**: promising, pleasant, solid, convincing, superb, impressive … **negative**: badly acted, infuriating, lousy, overacted, unconvincing, …

Thematic vocabulary: friendship – jealousy

	term	expressions	

friendship	friend
	friendship
	friendless
	friendliness
		a good/close/loyal
		  lifelong friend
		to make friends with sb.
		to be just (good) friends
		to stop being friends
		  with sb.
		an old friend of mine
		circle of friends
		to become friends
		to befriend sb.
		to be friends again
		to be friendly towards/
		  with sb.
		one of my best friends
		boyfriend/girlfriend/
		  schoolfriend
		a childhood/family
		  friend
			Topic:
			
			**friendship –
			jealousy**

jealousy	jealous
	jealously
		to feel jealous
		to make sb. jealous
		to get/become jealous
		jealous husband/wife/
		  lover/child
		a jealously guarded
		  secret	

Zum Klausurvorschlag Seite 160

Der folgende Klausurvorschlag erfordert eine Analyse der Szene 30 von *Dawson's Creek, episode 1, "Emotions in Motion" (33:59 – 35:47)*. Er geht davon aus, dass der Inhalt der Szenen 1 – 29 bekannt ist und die wichtigsten filmischen Gestaltungsmittel und deren Wirkung (wie in der Unterrichtsreihe beschrieben) vermittelt wurden (und Szene 30 noch nicht besprochen wurde).
Die Schüler sollten zunächst Gelegenheit erhalten, die Aufgaben und *annotations* zu lesen. Dann wird die Szene zweimal (mit kurzer Unterbrechung zum Schreiben) vorgespielt. Die Schüler machen sich während und nach dem Sehen Notizen.

Film scene: Dawson's Creek, episode 1, scene 30: "Dawson walks Jen home"

Assignments

1. Describe the situation Jen and Dawson find themselves in at this point in the story.
2. Analyse the cinematic devices the director employs in this scene to present Jen and Dawson as teenagers who have just fallen in love.
3. Choose one of the following assignments:
    a) Put yourself in Dawson's position at the end of this scene when he watches Jen leave. Write a voice-over text for him that reveals his feelings and thoughts at this moment.
    b) Put yourself in Jen's position at the end of this scene when she has entered her room. Write her diary entry of that day.

Annotations

to pounce: to move suddenly forward in order to attack
repulsive: very unpleasant
obnoxious: extremely unpleasant, in a way that offends
to pretend: to imagine that something is true

Possible solutions

1. At this point in the story Dawson has walked Jen home after a rather embarrassing night at the movies. Since he had agreed to Pacey's plan to invite Jen, and then had also asked Joey to come along, he feels responsible for the disastrous course the evening took. In scene 30 we see that Dawson and Jen are standing in front of Jen's house. She tells him that it was all her fault and they start talking openly. She says that she likes him and admits that she was unhappy in New York. They feel attracted to each other and would probably have kissed if Jen's grandma had not been watching. When Jen goes inside, Dawson watches her leave with a dreamy smile on his face.

2. Field size: medium long shot to show how they relate, close-ups of their faces to show their feelings, full shot to make the viewer aware of their body language
Point-of-view: alternating point-of-view shots, reverse angle shots to show how they respond to each other, over the shoulder shot to involve the viewer
Light, colours: soft colours, summer night, moonlight reflected on the still water of the creek, warm, soft lights in the house to create a romantic atmosphere
Sound: romantic music, crickets chirping to support the idea of a romantic night
Subtext: smiling faces, shining eyes, looking into each others' eyes, awkward movements to reveal the nervousness, intensity of the moment

3. a) What happened? I really think I'm in love with her. I've never met such a fantastic girl. I'm so happy, I'm not even angry at her grandma for interrupting us. I'm also going to pretend we kissed. It was so sweet of her to say that! And maybe we'll kiss tomorrow. But I can wait. We don't have to rush things.
Oh my God, this has never happened to me before. I have to tell Joey. – But Joey acted so weird tonight. I really don't know what got into her. Maybe it's not such a good idea to talk to her about my feelings for Jen. I better just go home and dream of Jen …

b) Dear diary,
Today was a memorable day. Our "double date" was very strange. Pacey disappeared to be with our teacher and Joey really embarrassed me with her stupid questions. She acted so weird when she saw that Dawson was holding my hand. You could think she is jealous. But she told me herself that she and Dawson are just good friends!? I don't understand why she doesn't like me.
But the most important thing is that Dawson held my hand in the theatre and walked me home. He is a great guy, I really like him. He's so shy, so sweet and sensitive (so unlike the guys I knew in New York). He even wanted to kiss me, but I couldn't because Grams was watching us. God, I really hope she'll see that he is not "the wrong kind of boy" for me. And I also hope that Joey will calm down and understand. I like her and I feel that we could be good friends. I'll talk to her tomorrow. … And to Dawson!

Acknowledgements

Jean Rhys, "I Used to Live Here Once". In Jean Rhys, *Sleep It Off Lady*, London: André Deutsch Ltd., 1976, S. 175 f.

Jerzy Kosinski: Documentary photographs. From: Jerzy Kosinski: Cockpit. Grove Press/Atlantic Monthly Press; Reprint May 1998, p 187 f.

Roger Karshner: Martha and Karen. A dramatic scene. From: Scenes they haven't seen by Roger Karshner. Dramatic publications 1983. Harbour Books, pp. 10–12

William Moseley: The split decision (excerpt). A short play. From: One-Act Plays for Acting Students, by Norman A. Bert. Meriwether Publishing LTD. Colorado Springs, Colorado 1987, pp. 74–77

Simon Armitage: I am very bothered. From: Simon Armitage: Book of Matches. Faber and Faber (UK), 2001 Book of Matches, Faber and Faber Ltd.

Jeremy Paxman: The British-American 'party'. From: Jeremy Paxman: *The English*. Penguin 1999, p. 40–42

Richard Ford: The question of Britishness that even had the Palace stumped. From: *The Times*, Tuesday November 1, 2005

Stephen Speight: Europe old and young (First edition)

Every effort has been made to supply complete copyright information for the texts included here. Should such entries be incomplete or contain errors, we request copyright owners to contact the publishers so that we can proceed with the necessary corrections.